CONGRATULATIONS!
YOU ARE A MANAGER!

CONGRATULATIONS! YOU ARE A MANAGER!

An Overview for the Profession of Manager

Lee E. Jacokes

authorHOUSE®

AuthorHouse™ LLC
1663 Liberty Drive
Bloomington, IN 47403
www.authorhouse.com
Phone: 1-800-839-8640

Published by AuthorHouse   09/13/2013

ISBN: 978-1-4918-0582-4 (sc)
ISBN: 978-1-4918-0581-7 (hc)
ISBN: 978-1-4918-0580-0 (e)

Library of Congress Control Number: 2013914270

Contents

Introduction

"By working faithfully eight hours a day, you may eventually get to be a boss and work twelve hours a day."

Robert Frost

How do most of us become managers? For many of us, it happens because we are good specialists. Because we are good at what we do, somewhere along the line, our superiors and our fellow specialists identify us as candidates for a managerial/supervisory position. Then, one day, we are one whether we are ready or not.

Some professions, such as medicine, psychology, ministry, and accounting, provide training and mentoring for those preparing for these careers. This training includes extensive formal education followed by an internship or practicum where the aspirants work along side practicing professionals for a period of time before being allowed into the profession. Unlike these professions, many, if not most, people enter management void of any systematized preparation for the position. Their preparation mainly consists of training in a specialty, for example, electrical engineering, sales or marketing, or quality control in manufacturing, and the lessons they learned through observing the managers they served under during their early career.

In promoting the specialist, an assumption is made that if the person is good as a specialist, he/she will be a good manager. What is true, however, is that taking on management/supervision duties plunges the new manager into a world demanding competencies not usually required in their specialties. The knowledge and skills needed to be a good manager are substantially different from those of a specialist.

Upon reflection, it seems ludicrous that managers are not given a more thorough preparation for their responsibilities as is true for other professions. These professions would not allow an under prepared person to enter the profession: however, this is the case with many managerial positions. This casual attention to preparation may also send a message that management is less important than other careers, underplaying the very serious nature and responsibilities management entails. Newly minted managers/ supervisors are given control over vital functions, including such areas as budgets, human resources, equipment, facilities, and other valuable resources. This "throw them into the pool and see if they can swim" approach can lead to unnecessary and costly mistakes.

What is it like to be a manager? There are undoubtedly as many answers to this question as there are managers since no one position is exactly the same as another. However, the reality of any position is a combination of many factors such as the job responsibilities, what the organization produces (products or services), the organization's climate and culture, the nature of the specialty being supervised, the experience and personality of the manager, and the economic conditions of the time.

Those aspiring to be managers often have a romanticized image of managerial life. Attracted by the prestige and power of management, they may not appreciate the seriousness, pressures, and challenges they will face. As you proceed through this book, five real life examples of the day to day experience of managers are presented. Review of these cases will give you a base of comparison to the managerial positions you are considering, or are presently occupying, and illustrate not only the specifics of each job but especially the common challenges every manager faces.

This book is directed toward those people who are considering a management career, have been recently promoted into such a position, or are already managers but have not had the opportunity to pursue a more formal managerial education. The book presents a short, concise coverage of essential things managers need to know.

The first section is a presentation of organizational culture and how cultural forces influence managerial success. Section 2 looks at the challenges of transitioning to management, focusing on the skills managers need. These skills include communication patterns, rational/non-rational forces supporting/restricting managerial actions, coping with conflict, and leadership challenges. Section 3 addresses several specific tasks all managers must handle such as planning, organizing, motivating, and controlling, as well as meetings, budgets, evaluation, and hiring and dismissal. Section 4 addresses the organization with a look at organizational design and organizational products and services. The book concludes with a look at the possibilities for continued professional managerial development.

This book will quickly introduce you to many of the complexities of the profession and help you anticipate challenges you will face as you learn on the job. As you proceed through these pages, you probably will experience the "I know that" phenomenon. Anyone who has a few years working in an organization collects many experiences and insights about the workplace. The variety of topics presented will help you bring more meaning and integration to those things you already "know."

It can be legitimately asked if a single book like this can address management as practiced in the variety of organizations ranging from profit and nonprofit, businesses and industry, social services and education, or government and religious organizations. The answer is yes. Management involves processes common to all types and sizes of organizations. The tasks faced by managers are far more common than unique, regardless of the organization's product/service or the specialties needed to run the organization. These similarities will become more apparent as we proceed.

Organizational Culture

"You can't always wait for the guys at the top. Every manager at every level in the organization has an opportunity, big or small, to do something. Every manager's got some sphere of autonomy. Don't pass the buck up the line."

Bob Anderson

One of the most influential but difficult to define characteristics in every organization is its culture. Analogous to individual personality, every organization develops its own culture. As a manager, you represent that culture, are expected to model its values, beliefs, and behaviors, and effectively communicate this culture to your subordinates. Understanding this culture, how it affects the work atmosphere, the direction it provides the organization, and its strengths and challenges is an important first step in your becoming a successful manager.

Organizational culture can be defined as "a pattern of shared basic assumptions learned by a group as it solved its problems of external adaptation and internal integration, which has worked well enough to be considered valid and, therefore, to be taught to new members as the correct way to perceive, think, and feel in relation to those problems" (p. 18).[1] Since each organization's history is different, its culture is a learned pattern of values and behaviors which comes to be unique to that organization.

You only need to visit different businesses and recognize the "feel" of each business as compared to the others. Even organizations within the same industry have different cultural characteristics and are experienced differently by their employees. It is these differences which make for both positive and negative characteristics. The culture incorporates the value structure and action assumptions upon which problem solving, decision making, and other organizational actions are based.

Discovering the Culture. Coming to understand an organization's culture is simultaneously easy and difficult. Consulting documents such as mission/vision/other public statements can reveal professed intentions and values. However, such public statements may or may not accurately reflect deeper cultural characteristics. Understanding these less public cultural elements can be achieved in other ways. Attending to organizational legends or stories praising the contributions of a revered founder/ employee can identify desired values or behaviors. Observing the organization's rituals such as how people are treated and are recognized/rewarded for their contributions and/or service can reveal the value placed on people. Symbolic artifacts can reveal cultural characteristics such as unique building architecture, office decor, workspace arrangements, status indicators, paintings and sculpture, etc.

Finding answers to questions as listed below can help you clarify underlying cultural values and assumptions influencing the organizations "personality."

- How is the status of employees determined?

- How are people of lesser status treated by higher ups?

- Is there a difference in dress code for different levels of employees?

- How are people at different levels addressed by people at other levels (Mr., Ms., Dr., Last name, First name)?

- How do employees treat one another?

- What are the performance expectations of employees?

- What position does the organization take toward profit, community involvement, religion, political attitudes?

- How does the organization deal with crises?

- How does the organization treat its customers?

- Is the organization open to suggestions, new ideas, and change?

- Is the organization family friendly?

- What reputation does the organization have in its community?

- Does the organization contribute to the life of the community?

- Is the atmosphere very formal or informal?

- How is the organization governed: directive/authoritarian, consultative, democratic?

- What criteria are used in selecting leaders/managers?

- Is the leadership honest and forthright?

- How do managers react to mistakes people make?

These and similar questions can be asked of your fellow employees, managers, organization leaders, former employees, and many others with experience and knowledge of the organization.

Leadership and Culture. Organizational culture is influenced by many sources such as the nature of the product/service provided by the organization; the culture of the country and community in which the organization resides; the background, education, and training of its workers; and so forth. However, leadership is the primary influence on organizational culture. To begin with, the founders infuse a long lasting imprint which incorporates their values, hopes, aspirations, and personal styles on the subsequent organizational climate. This impact can be felt even decades after they have passed. Subsequent leaders, often having been apprenticed to these founders, consciously and unconsciously adopt these values and behaviors, perpetuating both the good and bad. Later generations of managers may continue to be inspired by these cultural beliefs, values, assumptions, and behaviors. In fact, their promotion to management is partly influenced by their perceived adoption and support of the culture.

The culture is also influenced by subgroups representing specialists. Through their education, experience, professional values and standards, specialists such as accountants, engineers, nurses, teachers, sales persons, manufacturing workers, and union members bring their own set of standards, values, and behaviors. These specialists, in turn, create subgroup cultures which intermix with the broader organizational climate. These different subgroup values and behaviors bring important knowledge and skills to the organization but can also be the source of intergroup conflicts.

Thus, management and other employees influence and pass on the culture. Over time, people not at ease with the culture will either leave or be dismissed while those remaining are accepting/tolerant or "true believers." Such a selection process brings organizational stability and predictability but also can build in a strong resistance to changing outmoded and even harmful cultural characteristics. It is important to understand that not all cultural values are good or remain appropriate over time. A value of frugality may serve to keep expenses low and profits high but may prevent taking advantage of new technologies necessary to keep up with the competition. Companies which manage by intimidation may experience high turnover, loss of needed skills, reduced employee morale and productivity, and high employee replacement and training cost.

Since the organization has survived and prospered under its present culture, the attitude of "We have always done it this way" sets up a resistance to needed change. And, indeed, things do change. Technologies and processes improve, standards evolve, customers' expectations change, competition intensifies, all of which may require changes in some deeply embedded cultural elements. The challenge for you as a manager is to come to understand these cultural forces, understand their importance and limitations. Since many internal and external forces change over time, managers must realize when long held beliefs, assumptions, and behaviors are in need of modification and change.

How does a manager affect cultural change? Since cultural characteristics are deeply embedded, often collectively unconsciously held, it can be very challenging to change these elements. For example, let's assume the organization has a deeply

9

held belief in the importance of maximizing profit but also has a poor record of providing safe working conditions for its employees. To address the safety value may require diverting some of the valued profit toward improving safety conditions. To accomplish this shift in resources would require a modification of the profit value, a shift that may be strongly resisted. It would require the leadership/management to squarely face the problems and long term implications of a profit over safety values, with a solution that involves an acceptance of some reduction in profitability.

Another example of cultural change might be a departmental process of long standing which is no longer adequate for its original purpose. To improve this process, the introduction of new technologies and procedures becomes necessary. However, this will require redefining employee job descriptions and acquiring new knowledge and training, things that will be resisted by some employees because, "We have always done it this way!"

Cultural change involves a four step process. The first step is uncovering/recognizing the values, assumptions, or behaviors of the organization's culture. This requires a collective managerial ability for self reflection and critique, openness to criticism, and a willingness to seek external consulting assistance when necessary. Next it is important to revisit the historical origins of these values, assumptions, or behaviors. The third step is facing up to their limitations and importance. The final step is reconfirming, modifying, or discarding these values, assumptions, or behaviors as appropriate. As a manager, your familiarity with and ability to implement these four steps will help determine your success in your position.

As you take on the role of manager, you yourself affect the culture in which you work. If you are transitioning to manager in your current organization, you will be changing the nature of your relationships within that culture. Like all changes, this will require some adjustment on your part and on the part of your coworkers and management. If you are beginning your management responsibilities in a new organization, you need to become acquainted with that new culture, realizing that you are affecting this culture as a new manager. You need to be prepared for reactions to your new position from all levels of the organization. In the next section on Transitioning to Management, some of these issues will be addressed.

Transitioning to Management

"Leadership is not a position. You are not a leader because you have the title of manager. Leadership is something that we earn from followers on a day to day basis."

The EMS Manager Newsletter

Peer to Boss Transition

Advancement to a management or supervisory position is an important and joyful career event. Your family, friends, and colleagues are proud of you. The movement from peer to boss comes with increased responsibilities, prestige, and challenges. However, this transition is also fraught with potential difficulties and pain.

Shifting from peer to boss is a distinct role change not only from your perspective but also from the perspective of your former peers. Many fledgling managers experience the "Who am I" period in this role change. The new role creates a period of confusion in which the new manager is not sure if he/she is fish or fowl. That is, am I a friend or boss, a colleague or superior, a fellow worker bee or queen bee? This same confusion of role identity about your new manager role is also experienced by both your former peers and superiors who also are not quite sure how to relate to your new status. Some peers may perceive the former colleague as a traitor to the working class while former superiors may view the manager as an upstart or infiltrator from the workers. This difficulty in adjusting to your new status as manager is often revealed in good natured comments about the new manager or expressions of suspicions about motivations for accepting the promotion.

Promotion changes a fundamental factor affecting roles: the power difference between boss and subordinate. Power can be viewed from a managerial perspective as the ability of one person to influence the employment conditions of another. Since the new boss has such an advantage over the subordinate, you become a critical person in your subordinate's life. As a new manager you must come to understand this power difference and learn to use this power in appropriate ways. Often, managers have great difficulty in coming to grips with this new found influence over others. Some see it as an opportunity to produce needed changes while others use the power to pay back long held grievances. Still others shy away from power, refusing to recognize its legitimate uses, and fail to use it when needed. Recognition of the legitimacy of power and the need to use it appropriately is critical to effective management.

Two terms helpful in understanding changes in role relationships are: position power and personal power.[2] Position power refers to the amount of formal power delegated to a position including the power to hire and dismiss, to reward and punish, and to command obedience to follow orders. Personal power refers to the attributes of the manager holding the position such as personality characteristics, social background, education and experience, and relationships with superiors and other influential people in the work environment. These two power sources provide the legitimate and personal basis of influencing others.

The manager must understand that power is a temporary gift and not a permanent possession. Position power is delegated to the manager by virtue of the job's place in the formal hierarchy and can be taken away. Personal power is given by followers through the respect, admiration, trust, and confidence they have for the manager but can be withdrawn if the manager no longer deserves this respect. Thus, the manager must respect the temporary nature of power and use it wisely, fairly, and appropriately.

There are three scenarios or situations to which new managers may be promoted: promotion to lead a group of people who were fellow workers and peers, promotion to lead a group within the same organization but with whom you have had only casual contact, and promotion to lead workers with whom you have no prior knowledge and relationships. Each of these situations has its own unique challenges. Promotion from within your workgroup as its head can be the most difficult of the three scenarios. Before the promotion you were at a peer level, now you are their superior. Perhaps some of these former peers were also candidates for the promotion and may harbor hurt, embarrassed, or resentful feelings about your promotion or being passed over. Others may be happy and accepting of your elevation. In any case, all of your former relationships, friendships, antagonisms, conflicts, and feelings can become either supportive or hindrances to your new position. Not only do the former peers know your strengths and weaknesses but you know theirs also. All of these and other factors can lead to role confusion for both you and the former peers.

The new manager can expect initial difficulties as adjustment to the new role occurs. Examples of such behavior might include attempts to use your good feelings toward another to gain some advantage, hesitancy in approaching or relating to you, testing of your limits, and hostile behaviors. Others may be very cooperative and supportive of your new position and do all they can to assist you in your adjustment. You can count on a lot of good natured kidding about your new status, but underlying such comments are signs of their coming to terms with their new relationship to you and your/their roles.

What is your best approach to taking on the new position? There is probably no one best approach for everyone making this transition. You must be yourself, using your personal attributes. In general, count on your personal powers and relationships with former peers to ease you into the role. You should use position power and authority as appropriate, and respond to limit testing immediately. Do not be hesitant to let people know you are the boss when such testing occurs.

Appointment to head a group within the same organization can have similar challenges depending upon the group's prior contact and experience with you. Certainly, you can count on these new subordinates to "check you out" with your former peers before you arrive and have some predisposed notions of you. Adjusting to this new group will involve some of the same challenges as mentioned above. Again, count on your personal power to introduce yourself to the group, and assume that your newly delegated position power will be enough to allow you time to establish good relationships with your new subordinates.

Assuming leadership of a group unknown to you or you to them has its own characteristics. Since neither you nor your subordinates have prior experience with each other, the slate is clean and no prior relationships can either interfere or facilitate the relationships. Through the interviewing process, sharing of your resume and your past work history, some initial impressions are known; however, no other factors about your or their background is known. Since you start the job with the authority of the position, this is where you begin. You should formally introduce yourself to the group, share your background, and present your general expectations of the work group. Meet with each person over the next few days, asking them about their work background, experience, education and training, and their career goals. You should also share some similar information about yourself with the employee. During this process, you are not only gaining information about each person, you are beginning the process of establishing your position and personal power with each person. There is an old saying that the boss should establish a friendly, but not a friendship, relationship with subordinates. In assuming your new position, you must also be aware of role changes with your new fellow managers and superiors. They also will need time to adjust to your new relationship with them.

A concept helpful in understanding your relationships within the work environment is role set.[3] Any job is imbedded within an array of other positions including peers, subordinates, and superiors. A job's role set consists of all other positions in the work environment which depend upon the position holder to perform his or her job. All jobs are interconnected and have mutual dependencies with one another. In entering a new position, it is advisable that the new manager comes to know who belongs to his or her role set and makes an effort to know these people, know what they expect of the job, and how these people interact with the new manager's position. This can be determined by identifying each role set member and interviewing them to assess how they see the position, how they interact with the position, how the position affects them, and how they should communicate in the future. By taking the time to meet and talk with each role set member, the process of establishing both position and personal power with these members is started.

The importance of the initial relationship building process cannot be overstated. It represents the beginning of building trust and confidence between you and your colleagues. Both trust and confidence are necessary for the future development of a productive and supportive work environment. And remember, when the inevitable crises occur, these are the people you will have to depend upon. And, that is not the time to begin relationship building.

As you move into your new position, there are a number of roles you will be expected to fulfill depending upon the requirements of your position. Below are several roles you will need to understand and learn to perform.[4] These roles require unique combinations of the managerial knowledge and skills. As you review them understand that it will undoubtedly take time, perhaps years, to master them. The problem is that your subordinates and even other managers may expect you to be able to perform these roles on your first day!

Table 1: Management Roles and Definitions

Management Roles	Definitions
Interpersonal Roles	
Figurehead	Representing department/organization at ceremonial occasions, e.g. promotions, retirements, awards, funerals, etc.
Leader	Coordinating, directing, motivating, and controlling subordinates
Liaison	Contacting individuals/groups either internal or external to the organization to facilitate the work completion of the unit/department

Informational Roles	
Monitor	Scanning the environment for opportunities or threats which could affect the function/productivity of the work unit
Disseminator	Collecting and transmitting vital information to subordinates and other organizational members
Spokesperson	Speaking as a representative of the work unit to people either internal or external to the organization
Decisional Roles	
Entrepreneur	Improving the work unit by developing/adapting, and improving individual and group work processes and procedures for the work unit
Disturbance handler	Resolving conflicts and situations that destabilize the productivity and effectiveness of the work unit
Resource allocator	Allocating scarce resources to best accomplish the objectives of the work unit/organization
Negotiator	Negotiating with others to obtain needed resources for the work unit or organization

Developing the knowledge and skills required by the above responsibilities and roles requires your willingness to learn from knowledgeable and skilled professionals, integrate on-the-job experiences, and search out educational opportunities. In fact, developing these capabilities will be a career long challenge. This is how professionals become professionals.

Case Study: Lead Mechanic

Bob was in his second day as a lead mechanic and was wondering just what he got himself into. He had served as a jet engine mechanic for several years in a major commercial airline and had sought out this job with great anticipation. Now, he was having second thoughts. He was told to shadow two experienced Leads but was finding the experience to be of little help. Neither seemed willing to share their knowledge or help in his training. It was becoming abundantly clear that he was on his own to figure out what and how he was to function in his new role. He had watched others in this position over the years so had some feel for the job but it appeared little guidance was forth coming from either his new peers or his Foreman. "Sink or swim" was the apparent management training program. He did learn one thing quickly. Some Leads tried to dump their unwanted tasks on him, "the new kid on the block."

Bob reported to a foreman who reported to a manager who reported to the general manager of the maintenance division. Thus, Bob was far down the managerial pecking order. Bob was assigned eight mechanics to supervise, several of whom he had worked with previously. He found most of them supportive of his new role and appeared willing to accept his direction.

He started his day at about 5:15am and ended at 2:30pm. Upon arriving at work, he consulted the maintenance scheduling computer which identifies the progress of engine repair status including the priorities and progress of engine disassembling, part repair, and engine assembly. From this information he then assigned specific tasks to his mechanics prior to their arrival at 6:00am. At this time a brief meeting of all mechanics was held to assign tasks and present other company information, ending with a safety stretching exercise before work began.

At 7:00am a meeting of all foremen and lead mechanics was held to review and adjust work priorities for the day, discuss the next few days' engine repair plans, and present other work and company communications. Following this meeting, Bob attended to his other duties. Throughout the day he periodically checked on his subordinates' task performance and completion, assigning new tasks as others were completed, and provided other assistance such as making sure parts, tools, and other resources were available as needed. A surprising amount of time was spent on paper work to generate repair process orders, track the condition and repair status of engine parts, order parts and materials, and meet documentation requirements of the FAA.

As the weeks unfolded, Bob found the challenge of supervising, motivating, and disciplining employees to be more time consuming than he had anticipated. A few employees required significant amounts of time to insure they did their jobs. Newer mechanics required training while others required close supervision to see that they did their tasks rather than socializing or surfing the web. Also, communicating with people in other departments sometimes frustrated him because of their slow response in providing information and/or assistance needed for his group to accomplish their tasks on time.

After 18 months, Bob evaluated his transition into management as reasonably smooth. He felt his former peers readily accepted him as their boss with only one person giving him trouble. He continued to be disappointed with three of his fellow lead mechanics who were not supportive and continually attempted to off load their work on him. All in all, Bob enjoyed the challenge and excitement of his supervisory position. It called on him to use his specialized experience as a mechanic but challenged him to learn many new sets of knowledge and skills for which his previous experience had not prepared him.

Managerial Skills

All managers, whether at the top of the organization or at its lowest supervisory level enter their new management position with many questions such as:

- Do I have what it takes to succeed in this job?

- What knowledge and skills will I need to be successful?

- What type of organizational resources do I need to do this job?

- Will my fellow workers give the support I need to be successful?

Even those with no management experience usually come to a new position with some skills applicable to their new responsibilities. Most of life's endeavors require the use of basic management skills. Whether we are preparing for a trip, remodeling a home, managing a household, or planning our careers, use of management principles are often intuitively understood. Thus, you may already have a running start toward your new responsibilities.

To grow as a manager, you must continually develop three broadly defined skill areas: conceptual skills, human relation skills, and technical skills.[5] Conceptual skills involve the capacities to plan, problem solve, and apply other thinking processes. Human relation skills involve abilities to effectively communicate, form relationships, be sensitive to and motivate people. Technical skills refer to knowledge and skills related to the accomplishment of specific tasks. For example, nurses need patient care skills, engineers need mathematics knowledge, mechanics need mechanical aptitude, and computer analysts need programming skills.

Depending upon whether you are in top management, middle management, or supervision the exact combination of these skills will vary. Conceptual skills may be more involved in top management while technical skills may be more relevant at the supervision levels. Human relation skills are needed at all three levels of management. However, no matter the level of management, the appropriate knowledge and skills necessary for effective performance are critical.

Communication Patterns

> *"Effective managers spend 75% of their time listening and 25% of their time talking."* (Leadership Research Finding)

Information is critical to the functioning of all organizations and to your success as manager. How information is obtained, stored, retrieved, assessed, assembled into coherent messages, and then sent by the most reliable modes comprise the vast arena of organizational communication. Every aspect of a manager's success depends on effective communication of information. To carry out these responsibilities communication systems must permeate all basic functions of the organization; thus, making managerial functioning possible.

Information exchange involves not only person to person communication, but also other forms such as person to group, person to machine, machine to person, machine to machine, etc. Communication can be broken into two components: the processes by which information is sent and the content of the information. This section focuses on the processes inherent in organizational communication.

Communication involves interaction between two or more people or machines. Although there are vast differences between person to person and machine to machine communication, there are some similarities in their processes. The sender of information must retrieve the desired information from the brain or memory storage devise, compile it into a coherent message, and output the message through voice or other mechanisms. That message must pass through some medium such as air, paper, telephone, email, or other electronic media, and then be received by the receiver. The message receiver must in turn sense the message, correctly interpret the input, and understand the information.[6] The possibilities for faulty communication occurring along this complicated process are many. In fact the most frequently mentioned problem in most organizations is communication.

Communication effectiveness is also influenced by organizational structure. Formal structure is revealed by the typical line and staff chart (Figure 1, p. 89) which illustrates who reports to whom starting at the Board of Control and Chief Executive Officer (CEO) on down through divisions, vice presidents, department heads, etc. This structure not only spells out lines of authority and power but also defines the formal communication lines of the organization. Through the formal communication lines, detailed plans, goals, policies, orders, and directions are communicated. These formal communication lines have both advantages and disadvantages. Such communications are authoritative, can carry precise information, and act as the official word of the organization. Formal communication also can be slow in development and transmission throughout the formal structure. If only formal communication were allowed, it would be nearly impossible to get anything done.

Because the formal structure also implies each manager has the power to influence the well being of subordinates, communication upward can be distorted. Good news tends to become positively exaggerated while bad news tends to become less negative as it flows upward. No one wishes to be seen as the messenger of bad news. As information flows toward the top, tendencies to "wash" information for fear of looking poorly to one's superior, may cause the information to become less exact and accurate, which in turn can lead to poor decisions. The guy or gal at the top may be the last to know the real truth. The potential negative effects of the formal power/communication structure have been dramatically revealed by investigations into airline crashes, space shuttle disasters, and medical errors in hospitals. In these situations, the reluctance of subordinates to challenge incorrect judgments of their superiors was found to be a contributing cause of these disasters. Though few managers face such critical situations, it is important to be aware that your subordinates may have difficulty saying things clearly, passing on unwelcome information, and critiquing you when your judgments may be incorrect. The wise manager must encourage open communication, listen non-defensively, evaluate employee ideas, and not punish employees for honest, well intentioned critique. Without clear communication and openness to ideas, your probability of success as a manager will be considerably reduced.

To make tasks easier, lateral communication occurs. Lateral communication takes place between people who do not formally report to one another. This is necessary because tasks tend to flow laterally within and between vertical divisions of the organization. Workers within a department rely upon one another to complete tasks. If they had to go to their supervisor above them to communicate to one another, as the formal chart would suggest, this would take longer to complete than if they simply directly communicate with each other. Lateral communication contains both formal and informal elements. Information related to task completion is formal but non task communications also occur. These non task related interactions range from exchange of daily pleasantries to news of the day and the latest sports results, to the current company gossip, to arranging gatherings at the local watering hole after work, and exchange of many other non task related communications. This interaction promotes the development of informal communications and relationships. These non task communications are the foundation of the informal communication networks in all organizations.

All people have varying needs for social interaction and the work place is an important source for meeting that need. Employees form all types of informal networks to help meet their social needs ranging from forming close personal relations with fellow workers, to joining the bowling and softball team, to being part of the infamous grapevine. These are normal activities and take place with or without formal organizational approval. Underpinning any organization is a web-like set of both formal and informal networks which support the work of the organization and, at times, can create problems. Informal communication is frequently much faster at relaying information throughout the organization; however, the information may or may not be accurate since there is no check on its validity or accuracy.

Thus, factual information as well as gossip and rumors can pass throughout the informal network. Each organization must find the correct balance between formal and informal communication processes without stifling either. Relying on the formal systems too tightly can result in a stultifying and impersonal work environment. Attempting to crush informal communication will result in poor work production, will inhibit creativity, and will drive the informal communication "underground." Letting informal communication become the dominant communication mode will produce communication chaos.

Effective organizational communication is not only a product of formal and informal networks but also is profoundly influenced by individual communication abilities and motivations. One's ability and motivation to share and communicate information varies greatly between individuals. Some people communicate freely and articulately while others hoard and/or restrict information. The capacity to evaluate incoming information, to understand its meaning and importance, and to decide and formulate messages to share with others, is fundamental to effective communication. Thus, one's inherent communication capacities have a profound impact on the amount and clarity of information the individual can communicate.

People also vary in their motivation to communicate. Some individuals use information as a power tool, restricting information because it represents a forceful commodity which elevates them to a position of importance and influence. Holding onto information places them in a position of organizational power and influence—a person to be reckoned with when their information is needed by others. Other individuals use their possession of valuable information as a means of gaining attention and prestige among fellow workers. After all, if you know things others want to know and are willing to share it, you may be perceived as an important and influential person. Most people are not at the extremes presented above, but have reasonable skills and judgments about what and when information should be shared. If the person you need information from in order to do your work is unable or unwilling to share, this reduces your ability to effectively do your job no matter how well structured the communication networks are. As a manager, it is important to know the communication abilities of those with whom you work. With this understanding, you can become more effective in communicating with and through others. To be an effective manager, you need to form good relationships with superiors, peers, and subordinates, establishing support for your unit. Such relationships are dependent upon you being an effective communicator.

In former times, information resided exclusively in paper files or in the memories of employees. This is still true; however, the advent of electronic information systems brings another complication to organizational communications. The availability and accessibility of this information is also critical to effective information exchange. Though this is not the place to delve into information system details, it is essential that you have a basic understanding of computers. You must be able to type (by touch or sight, with two or more fingers, by elbow or nose) in order to function. So many organizational processes are computerized that it is now impossible to be effective without some computer knowledge and skills. You must develop knowledge and skills to use the variety of electronic communication tools such as e-mail, word processing, software specific to tasks of the organization, and one's technical specialty. The rapidity of communication is also influenced by cell phones, instant messaging, and even Facebook and Twitter!

Thus, organizational communication is complicated and difficult to manage and control because it includes the entire organization, its formal and informal networks, the variety of electronic and computer technologies, and all the individual communication abilities and motives of employees. There are many other aspects to effective communication. However, the above factors are a start to understanding the vital role communication and information play in your success as a manager.

Case Study: Lead Production Superintendent

Senior Master Sergeant Mark had a problem. He was short two fighter jet planes. His air force base was responsible for training jet fighter pilots and, as Lead Production Superintendent for his fighter squadron of 260 Air Force personnel, he was responsible for making sure each plane in his 26 plane inventory was flight ready to support their training missions.

To accomplish this task Mark was supported by personnel in eight support specialties including wash (corrosion control), fueling, ordinance/weapons, avionics (radar, communications), electrical, engines, hydraulics, sheet metal, and machine shop. The squadron duty officer who communicated these specifications to Mark on a weekly basis determined pilot training needs. These training needs drove Mark's and his colleagues' activities for that week. Tomorrow, pilot training required 20 planes configured to the specific training needs of each pilot such as fuel tanks and weapons. Thus, Mark must alert appropriate specialty heads how each plane was to be equipped for the day's flight needs and see that each plane was ready to fly when needed.

Since planes were flown nearly each day, they must be continually inspected for difficulties. Many factors negatively impact plane maintenance including the normal day to day stress and strain of flying, weather conditions, and the age of the plane. Thus, continual inspection for problems occurred on a daily basis. After each plane returned from a training sortie, pilots were debriefed about the plane's performance while the maintenance crew chief inspected for problems. If the plane checked out, it was certified for flight; however, if problems were detected, this information was entered into the plane's data base maintenance record and the information was sent to Mark. He in turn reviewed the plane's record, determined what repairs were needed, alerted the appropriate specialty of the plane's repair needs, and dispatched the required specialist or sent the plane to the appropriate area for repair. Mark also determined how long the repair should take and adjusted the flight ready plane roster to reflect plane availability. He also inspected the past maintenance record to determine if any chronic problems were evident. If so, he instructed the involved specialty to investigate and solve the underlying cause of the problem.

Though 20 jets were needed for tomorrow's sorties, only 18 were ready to fly leaving him two planes short. Usually, 2 ready to fly planes were held in reserve to cover unexpected breakdowns. However, of the 8 planes supposedly available, two were in extended repairs, two were in mandatory preventative maintenance, and 4 were undergoing less extensive repair. Mark reviewed the progress of these 4 planes and decided to put extra personnel on a plane with less involved repairs. This plane was made ready for flight by the next day's flight time, leaving Mark short only one plane for that day. Mark began his typical 10 to 12 hour day at the daily 6:00am production meeting. He updated his superiors about the repair and readiness status of each of the squadron's 26 planes, of his solution to today's plane shortage, the lack of one plane for today's training needs, and how the lost training time was to be made up given the status of plane maintenance.

Mark considered the biggest challenge of his job to be anticipating problems and acting before they became major difficulties. Knowing each plane's maintenance history, its performance under typical training demands, and then projecting probable maintenance needs before they became emergencies were essential to keeping planes in the air.

Mark's position served as a critical communication hub for the many people involved in plane maintenance and determining training needs. Mark received information from crew chiefs, the duty officer, and specialty heads. He communicated plane conditions to the various maintenance specialties and informed others of the flight readiness of each plane. He must be computer literate, using information necessary to assess plane conditions, and make critical decisions about the flight readiness of each plane.

Rational and Non-Rational Factors in Management

We tend to view management as a rational and logical process. However, managership has not only logical components but also emotional and social forces which influence decisions. In fact, some of these forces are down right irrational.

The case of the Challenger Space Shuttle disaster illustrates some of these forces. On January 28, 1986 just over one minute after lift-off, Challenger exploded due to an engineering flaw in the design of fuel tank O ring seals, killing all seven crew members. Investigation into the causes of the event found that NASA's organizational culture and decision making processes were contributing factors to the disaster. To begin with, the design flaw was known since 1977 to both engineering and management personnel but nothing was done to correct the potential catastrophic flaw. Managers also failed to respond to warnings about the cold temperatures on the morning of the launch and the temperature's impact on decreasing the O rings' effectiveness. The investigation pointed to the engineering group's failure to adequately communicate the criticalness of the temperature problem, the impact of pressure from management to have a successful on-time launch, and all around lack of effective communication. Other contributing pressures included a resistance toward incurring the enormous cost involved in redesigning the O rings, NASA's aggressive schedule of missions to meet income needs, the pressure from congress to limit funding, the desire on the part of NASA officials to meet the expectations of the media and public for support, and the desire to project an image of effectiveness of the manned space efforts. This case illustrates the impact both internal and external factors have on managerial decision making.

Have you ever wondered about your own organization and asked questions such as:

- Why do managers sometimes make stupid decisions?

- Why do the lazy and incompetent occasionally get rewarded while the dedicated and competent get ignored?

- Why do certain organization subgroups gain influence over others while other groups get trampled upon?

- Why do good ideas get ignored and bad ideas get embraced?

To answer such questions, we need to understand both the rational and non-rational components of managerial and organizational life.

The rational components of management can be seen in the logical ways in which we plan and organize[7] the work of the organization. We set goals, develop the necessary policies, processes, and standards needed to produce products and/ or services, organize all of these activities into a coherent organizational structure, fitting all these components into a logical pattern geared to producing our desired outcomes. In this way we design or engineer[8] the needed components into a type of "machine" which, once set in motion, will produce the outcomes we desire. Management's job is to see that the machine completes its work in an acceptable manner. The hope is that this organizational machine will continue to turnout its product or service perfectly. However, there is a variable complicating this hope: people. Organizations are also social systems; that is, they are influenced by internal individual, group, social, and environmental forces[9] which can both facilitate or alter the machine's intended purpose.

Personal Characteristics. Unlike machines, people come to their jobs with many different personal characteristics. They have different abilities, interests, education, work experiences, motivations, and needs. They bring their ethnicity, gender, personal histories, and outside interests. In other words, they are diverse human beings with a wide variety of motivations, goals, and behaviors. They may or may not share the same work motivations as the owners and managers. Some may see their job as a means to advancing their personal careers; others may be on the job only for the pay and seek outside activities for life fulfillment. However, as much as the organization tries through its control and motivation systems, these factors lead to less than perfect machine - like performance. These personal attributes play a major role in how any organization performs.

Social Factors. In addition to their personal characteristics, people are social creatures. They form friendships with fellow employees and divide themselves into informal groups. Management arranges them into work groups and departments, and they belong to management, professional, and craft specialties, or unions. In this social environment, people come together for mutual self interests, to represent a point of view, and to achieve common goals. These groups create their own membership expectations, pursue their own objectives, and influence organizational direction for their own benefit. Such group dynamics can be the cause of many subgroup interactions, some of which may cause managers to behave in ways neither rational nor beneficial to the goals of the organization.

Political Forces. Though many people complain about the existence of "politics," it is a reality which affects every manager. Politics is neither good nor bad. Just as a hammer can be used for both constructive and destructive purposes, so can politics. At its roots politics is about power and influence over others: the capacity to influence others to accommodate one's needs, wants, and goals. The influence sought involves the use of both position and personal power discussed earlier. At the individual level this includes establishing an authority position over others and/or developing personal connections with those who do exercise power. At the group level, the force of the group's goals, of its collective membership and ability to persuade others, is the basis of its influence.

These group dynamics lead to the political interactions present in every organization. Political influences primarily revolve around personal ambition, ideology, resource competition, and subgroup dynamics. People come to the work setting with convictions to which they hold strongly. These ideologies can take the form of ethical principles, leadership philosophies, profit assumptions, approaches to customers, assumptions about work performance, the role of union/management interactions, to name a few. People have a way of finding those with similar views and working together to promote their mutual self interests.

It is the rare organization that has unlimited resources. Because resources are limited, competition for dollars, people, and physical resources is inevitable. This can result in individuals and groups competing for these resources, influencing the keepers of such resources, and attempting to control them for their own purposes. Additionally, the dynamics of organizational subgroups can be the source of political maneuvering. Those subgroups which are change oriented can clash with those charged with maintenance of organizational stability. For example, sales is charged with selling to customers and will try to accommodate customer needs and wants; however, production is charged with keeping quality high and costs low, and is resistive to accommodating customer needs and wants for fear of interfering with these directives.

Non-Rational Factors in Decision Making. Managers face many complex problems in directing and running an organization. Faced with these complexities, sometimes less than optimal problem solving and decision making occurs. This limitation on the rationality of decision making is sometimes referred to as "bounded rationality."[10] Those making decisions can suffer from several limitations. They can look at a problem in a dichotomous manner (black and white terms, good or bad, right or wrong mentality), not understanding that nearly all problems have multiple causes. Such simplistic thinking fails to uncover root causes and understand how these causes are interrelated, ending in a decision which fails to address these causes. There may be a desire to simplify the problem, to be driven by time pressures, by the need to save time and money, or just to get the problem "out of your hair."

The failure to use known problem solving methods by accepting the first solution which comes to mind often leads to bad decisions. Excessive use of the formal authority structure can limit innovative problem solving. Political or influential sources may force decisions on managers which they might not make in other circumstances. Personal relationships may influence decisions contrary to good decision making or just plain blackmail may raise its ugly head.

Environmental Factors. Another source of factors is external environmental conditions. These conditions include such forces as government regulations, economic conditions, social/cultural values, physical environmental characteristics, information availability, and technology. These external forces both facilitate and restrict what organizations can and cannot do. In the case of the Challenger disaster, many of the above mentioned forces played a part in impairing the decision making processes of NASA.

Though most of us do not manage activities with such life and death consequences as NASA, our daily activities and decisions are influenced by such forces. So what can you as a manager do to address all of these personal, social, political, environmental, and non-rational factors? First, be aware they exist and concentrate on those that you can influence. The various management control systems, to be discussed later, can be viewed as means by which this variety of human variability can be reduced and directed. This variability reduction is necessary for any organization to function and be productive. Without such controls people would have no direction and would act in chaotic ways. On the other hand, if too much control is exerted, human beings become bored, resistive, hostile, demoralized, and non-productive. It is a balance that is needed: a balance which maximizes the advantages of a well planned and designed organization with human concerns which maximize and address the potential and ingenuity of people. Establishing such a balance is the challenge of a good manager and an optimized organizational system.

Competition and Conflict

Among the many factors managers must facilitate is the fact that people do not always get along and may find themselves in disagreement, leading to personal animosity and/or group conflict. As a manager, you will undoubtedly be required to referee such situations. Basically, inherent in personal and political interactions is the possibility of competition and conflict. Some potential situations for competition and conflict include: goals may collide; personalities and egos clash; groups struggle over power sharing, over limited resources, or clash over subsystem dynamics. The difference between competition and conflict is sometimes difficult to determine since the line between them is often blurred and indistinct.

Competition suggests a contest between parties (individuals and/or groups) where one side tries to best the other over some desired outcome. Both parties follow some generally understood or specifically recognized set of rules which provides both guidelines and limitations to what types of behaviors are allowed each party. Thus, sports teams follow rules and regulations relative to the specific sport; sales groups attempt to sell more product than another group; departments compete with one another to produce the highest quality product or have the best safety record, etc.

The "rules" prevent each competitor from behaving in ways that limit each other from undermining the other's attempt to "win the game."

On the other hand, conflict suggests a more ominous process in which there are few or no rules limiting behaviors. Not only do parties compete but they may also attempt to block, impede, interfere with, and overcome each other in ways that leave the opponent incapacitated and, in the extreme, demolished. Thus, conflict may result in the defeat, demoralization, and elimination of the other. Warfare is the extreme example of conflict.

Competition and conflict are present in all organizations at one time or another. Competition and conflict can be positive forces within the organization leading to improved processes and performance, unearthing previously unrecognized internal stress lines and forcing innovation to address these conditions. However, if ignored, both can lead to destructive consequences such as undermining the productivity and effectiveness of the organization, dividing employees into antagonistic factions, creating employee morale issues, and fostering a conflict prone culture.

In managing competition and conflict, the first challenge is to become aware of their presence, what the issues are, and who the significant participants are. This is not always easy, since participants may try to hide their involvement in these activities, especially when the conflict is to their advantage. Keeping competition and conflict within constructive bounds and intervening to prevent destructive behavior is one of your responsibilities as a manager. Though confronting conflict is not a pleasant responsibility, to ignore it and let it fester is to allow a cancer to grow with potentially devastating consequences for the organization and its employees.

To understand competition and conflict, one perspective to consider is the love-hate continuum of interpersonal relations. Love occurs when parties have great affection, respect and admiration for one another, and would do everything to accommodate and assist the other party no matter what the situation. On the hate end of the dimension, individuals and groups despise all others, consider the others as obstacles and enemies to their cause, and would do anything to overcome/defeat the others. In-between these two extremes are several combinations of love-hate attitudes and behaviors.

Paralleling this continuum are types of strategies to facilitate the love-hate relationships. For each point on this continuum there is a strategy for managing competition and conflict. In fact, these strategies can be viewed as means to solving a problem, even if the solution is one of destroying the other party. The following are examples of strategies used to resolve relationships on the love-hate continuum.

1. Self Sacrifice/Love. Conflict between two persons or groups is resolved by one party sacrificing their own needs in favor of meeting the other party's needs, thus setting aside their own needs and/or position. A soldier falling on a grenade to save fellow soldiers is an extreme example. In organizational terns, this would mean sacrificing one's own position in favor of another. An example would be one department forgoing a needed budget increase because of the needs of some other department. Another example would be workers agreeing to take less pay as a means of preventing layoffs of fellow workers.

2. Mutual Cooperation/Collaboration. This strategy involves both parties in mutual creative problem solving by finding conflict solutions which satisfy both parties. For example, a conflict between trying to meet the needs of a customer without requiring an expensive change in the production process might be solved by sales and manufacturing finding a new method of meeting both needs without disruption to normal processes.

3. Compromise/Negotiation. This approach looks to defining solutions which give each party some of what they seek

but probably not satisfying either party fully. Each party gets part of what they wanted but must give up something to do so. Sharing an increase in budget allocation between two departments when each wanted the entire allocation for themselves is an example.

4. Political Maneuvering. In this strategy, the conflicting parties are not interested in finding mutual solutions but look for ways of achieving their goals even if it means disadvantaging the other party. An example is members of one party influencing decision makers to allocate needed financial resources entirely to themselves rather than other deserving departments.

5. Warfare: Covert or Overt. This strategy focuses on the total defeat and/or elimination of the other party no matter what the inflicted harm. Warfare involves the deliberate use of political power, deception, and/or coercive force to defeat the opposing party at any cost. An example is a hostile takeover of one company by another.

Competing/conflicting parties seek to win and avoid losing.[11] The table below presents four possible outcomes. Both parties can enjoy a win-win solution, a win-lose or a lose-win solution, or a lose-lose result.

Table 2: Resolution Strategies for Conflict Management

Individual or Group A

		WIN	LOSE
Individual or Group B	**WIN**	WIN:WIN • Self Sacrifice • Collaboration • Compromise/Negotiation	LOSE:WIN • Compromise/Negotiation • Political Maneuvering
	LOSE	WIN:LOSE • Compromise/ Negotiation • Political Maneuvering	LOSE:LOSE • Political Maneuvering • Warfare

These four possible outcomes are dependent upon the motivations and resolution strategies employed by each party. The list of strategies given above shows those strategies most likely to lead to the specific combined outcomes and suggests to managers which strategies are to be considered depending upon the outcome desired.

From an organizational perspective, strategies which lead to win-win results are most desirable. Thus, the first three strategies are the most likely to lead to both parties gaining and neither party losing. Further, the resulting solutions from these three strategies can increase the probability that the conflict remains permanently resolved rather than creating long term hidden problems associated with political or warfare strategies.

Because conflicting parties are often unable or unwilling to directly interact with one another, as manager, you must be the one to confront the warring parties and require them to participate in conflict resolution processes. You may personally lead the resolution efforts or may need to consult with trained conflict resolution professionals. As with other managerial skills, knowledge and experience in conflict resolution are available through written materials, training, and workshops.

Leadership

> *"Efficiency tends to deal with Things. Effectiveness tends to deal with People. We manage things, we lead people."*
> (Unknown)

In assuming a management or supervisory position, you also take on a leadership role. Leadership occurs in many arenas, for example, community, political, social, military, business, and religious contexts. Management can be viewed as a subset of leadership in which you take on the responsibility to lead followers to meet the goals of the organization and its subunits.

Efforts to understand the nature of leadership have been pursued for centuries, ever since the first humans began to work together in groups. Three general leadership concepts have emerged over the years: trait, behavioral, and situational explanations.

Trait Definitions. Trait explanations suggest that people become leaders because they possess a unique set of personal characteristics including intelligence, motivation, personality traits, physical capabilities, and so forth, which combine to produce a leader. This approach is probably the most common held idea of leadership. For example, a person may be a charismatic leader, possessing abilities to attract, motivate, and convince people to follow his/her ideas. Trait definitions suggest that leadership is a possession of the individual, occurring because of these personal qualities. If it is possible to identify people with these qualities, they are more likely to become good leaders than those lacking these qualities. Though several traits have been found in a majority of successful leaders[12], the fact that some leaders do not possess these traits suggests their possession is not absolutely necessary to be a good leader. For example, even if a majority of leaders are extroverts there are many introverts who are effective leaders.

Behavioral Definitions. Behavioral explanations consider leadership the result of learned behaviors which give structure and support to followers. Through education, training, and experience, the leader can acquire the knowledge and skills necessary to become a good leader. Thus, this suggests any person can learn how to be a leader if motivated to do so.

Situational Definitions. Situational leadership explanations consider leadership as a result of external, environmental forces outside of the leader. These situational influences include such factors as time pressures, follower abilities and motivations, economic conditions, management-union-employee relations, availability of resources, and the type and amount of personal and position power held by the leader. These and many other factors can either help or hinder the efforts of any leader regardless of their personal traits or learned behaviors. Effective leadership is therefore heavily influenced by these environmental forces.

All three of these approaches explain some aspects of leadership and are therefore important to your understanding of leadership. A critical point to understand is that leadership is a complex system of interacting forces including the personal and learned characteristics and behaviors of the leader, the characteristics of followers, and the environmental forces acting upon both leader and followers. Three leadership examples particularly helpful for new managers are explained below.

Transformational/Transactional Leadership. This explanation defines two general types of leaderships.[13] Transformational leadership occurs when the leader leads followers toward a higher level of performance, often toward change which leads to new horizons. This type of leadership is future and change oriented, moving followers to a higher reality. Transactional leadership occurs when leaders work with followers to accomplish routine tasks required for the normal operations of the department/

organization. Transactional leadership is sometimes referred to as management, reserving the term leadership for transformational efforts. However, whether one heads an entire organization or a small number of followers, both types of leadership are needed. For example, the president of a company may lead the company into a new market resulting in significant growth while the manager of a unit may introduce new processes and technologies to modernize a unit's work flow. Both of these efforts are transformational.

Situational Leadership. An interesting and practical model is Situational Leadership developed by Hersey and Blanchard[14] which includes personal characteristics, learned behavior, and situational factors. The model is easy to learn and a good foundation for understanding leadership. The model suggests that each of us has a basic leadership style consisting of two factors: task behaviors and relationship behaviors. This basic style is developed due to a combination of our personal traits and the examples of leadership we experienced from our parents and other authority figures.

Task behaviors consist of leader actions which define tasks, work schedules, performance standards, time parameters, and other behaviors which structure follower actions toward accomplishing work tasks. Relationship behaviors consist of leader behaviors which motivate followers through such actions as rewards, encouragement, morale building, and recognition for a task well done. Leaders can vary in the amount of either task or relationship behaviors resulting in one of four leadership styles: High Task/Low Relationship (Style 1 - Telling), High Task/High Relationship (Style 2 - Selling), Low Task/High Relationship (Style 3 - Participating), and Low Task/Low Relationship (Style 4 - Delegating).

An S1 - Telling style would emphasize high amounts of directive and structuring actions including close supervision, frequent appraisal, providing instructions about how a task is to be performed, checking on follower performance, critique of actions, and high expectations of performance. At the same time, this leadership style would provide little relationship behaviors, low encouragement, recognition, rewards, etc. In extremes, this style of leadership could be described as a slave driver leadership style. An S2 - Selling style has a high amount and variety of task and relationship behaviors. In addition to the task behaviors described above, relationship behaviors would include a high amount and variety of encouragement, recognition, praise, and emotional support. S3 - Participating style has low task but high relationship behaviors. Carried to extremes, this style could be described as the laidback, easy going approach. Finally, S4 - Delegating style provides low amounts of both task and relationship behaviors. Carried to an extreme, this approach could end up as a hands off style, where little or no direction or encouragement would be given to followers.

Each of the four styles has both strengths and weaknesses. S1 - Telling can be helpful in providing proper direction but stifling if carried to extremes. S2 - Selling can provide both direction and encouragement but can be an obstacle to letting followers become more independent and self sufficient. S3 - Participating can recognize and encourage growing expertise but never let the follower develop confidence to assume responsibility. S4 - Delegating can let followers work independently but not provide help and assistance when given unfamiliar tasks. So, the good news is that whichever one of these styles is your basic style, that is fine. The bad news is that style is not enough.

Why is your basic leadership style not enough? Because, followers differ in their "Readiness" levels depending upon the tasks required of them. Readiness level is the situational component to this leadership model. The concept of readiness level recognizes that followers vary in their ability (competence) and willingness (motivation) to do a specific task. Depending upon a follower's readiness level for a specific task, the type of leadership style needed changes. A person new to a task will need considerably more direction, training, and supervision than another follower who has the necessary training and experience to do the task. Thus, the follower's needs (readiness) determine the leadership style. The model suggests that excellent leaders must change styles to meet follower needs. It is not sufficient for the leader to use his/her basic style for every follower if the follower needs a different leadership style. The leader must be style flexible, be able and willing to move to the style most appropriate to the readiness level of the follower.

Readiness is conceived as a continuum ranging from low readiness to high readiness. A low readiness level (R1—unable and unwilling or insecure) is followed by three increasingly higher readiness levels (R2—unable but willing or confident, R3—able but unwilling or insecure, R4—able and willing or confident). When assigning a task, the leader must first determine the follower's readiness level for the task. This determines the leadership style needed by the follower for this specific task. Thus, each readiness level is matched to a specific leadership style (R1 to S1, R2 to S2, R3 to S3, and R4 to S4). The leader must use the leadership style matched to the follower's designated readiness level for the best results.

In determining a subordinate's readiness level, both the competence (ability) level to do the task and the person's willingness/motivation level must be determined. In short the leader must consider the follower's ableness and willingness to do the task and then select the appropriate leadership style. It is important to note that a specific task must be evaluated, not the overall general ability and willingness of the follower. A person may be quite able and willing (R4) to do one task and need little or no direction and encouragement (S4) but when assigned an unfamiliar task may lack the knowledge, skills, and confidence/willingness (R1) and will need greater direction and supervision (S1). Failure to provide the appropriate leadership style can have unanticipated and negative consequences. A person needing more S1 - Telling behavior but given an S4 - Delegating style, can become very frustrated and discouraged. On the other hand, a person perfectly able to be delegated a task but given close supervision and told how to do a task already known well, can end up being frustrated and angry and have his/her confidence level undermined. Miss-matched style and readiness levels can lead to poor performance and demoralization for the follower. It is the needs of the follower which should guide the manager in providing the necessary leadership intervention.

Servant Leadership. Another concept of leadership is Servant Leadership.[15] This definition of leadership proposes some people are motivated toward leadership because they wish to serve others rather than motivated by the desire for power and material success. As a leader their focus is assisting others to grow, mature, and become healthier, free, autonomous, and more likely to become servant leaders themselves. To influence the growth and well-being of others suggests that effective leaders view their position as one of servant not lord and master. Thus, the servant leader provides appropriate direction, support, encouragement, structure, and resources to his/her followers which facilitate the subordinates' work efforts. If these qualities are provided to subordinates then the subordinates will respond in a favorable manner.

Your Leadership Challenge. Fundamentally, most people need certain basic conditions to be successful on a job. These conditions are necessary knowledge, direction, motivation, and skills to do their job, and a safe, supportive environment in which to work. The challenge for you as manager is to do your best to provide/encourage these conditions for your followers. This will require you to understand and use the personal traits you bring to the management table, recognize your strengths and limitations, strive to acquire the necessary knowledge and skills needed to be a good leader, and understand the facilitating and inhibiting environmental/organizational forces which will influence your success as a manager/leader.

Case Study: Manufacturing Superintendent

Jack arrived in his superintendent position in an office furniture manufacturing plant by an unanticipated and indirect route. He started his career in cost accounting followed by a stint as a human resource specialist, both of which required him to be on the assembly floor working with managers and hourly workers. During that time he became enthralled with the fast pace, the energy and excitement of the manufacturing process. He decided he would like to manage in this challenging environment. After a rigorous assessment process he was assigned to supervise a machine room. Initially, he was viewed with suspicion by his subordinates on two accounts: he had not come up through the manufacturing ranks and he was identified as an "HR" guy—how could he know anything about machines and what it took to supervise hourly people? He won worker respect by clearly communicating his expectations and earning their trust and confidence by treating them as competent adults and recognizing their contributions to the success of the department.

After two years, he was promoted to a superintendent position. He reported to the plant manager and had six supervisors reporting to him. They in turn supervised about 150 hourly workers. His assembly area involved three processes: cutting fabric, attaching fabric to fiberglass material, and assembling these parts into an office panel.

Jack characterized his responsibilities as "managing the process." Defining the process were six general goals to be attained: budget control, cost reduction, quality control, labor efficiency, on-time customer schedule completion, and health and safety. Jack typically arrived at work at 6:30am and began by reviewing the previous day's production performance metrics for schedule completion, cost containment, quality targets, and safety. This was followed by a "start up" meeting with the supervisors to review the above metrics, assess today's production goals, and determine possible difficulties which might interfere with meeting these goals such as equipment problems, missing parts, personnel shortage, etc. Much of his day was spent in problem solving for such issues as personnel problems, improving employee relations, and addressing conditions related to meeting production goals in a timely, cost effective, quality manner. The remainder of the day was involved in meetings with individuals and groups to discuss and develop approaches for continuous improvement and reducing costs and overhead.

One of the most difficult challenges of the job was laying off valued employees when customer orders declined. He worried about how these layoffs hurt the employee and his/her family as well as the loss of expertise to the company. Yes, the job could be stressful; however, it was this variety of activities and immediacy of performance that attracted and energized Jack.

Jack's transactional leadership qualities were well appreciated by both his superiors and subordinates, reflected in his promotion to plant manager after 3 years as superintendent. In this role, he exemplified transformational leadership abilities by introducing significant changes in plant structure and processes. He initiated a reorganization of the assembly process, introducing cross training, job rotation, employee involvement processes; changed the compensation system from piece work to hourly wages; and consolidated several manufacturing sites into a more cost efficient and productive environment.

And what makes a good manager? Jack summarizes his answer to this difficult question by indicating the manager must clearly communicate his/her goals and expectations and prove through behavior that you care about your subordinates. You must be willing and able to provide the necessary resources to accomplish their jobs and assist and support them. With such attention, people are willing to follow you and give you support.

Management Tasks

Don't be a time manager, be a priority manager. Cut your major goals into bite-sized pieces. Each small priority or requirement on the way to the ultimate goal becomes a mini goal in itself.

Denis Waitley

Management tasks are known at some level to most everyone. Most of the projects undertaken in a lifetime require the use of basic management principles. Whether preparing for a vacation, landscaping the yard, or planning for the future, application of management principles is often intuitively understood. In attempting to accomplish any activity it is necessary to set goals and objectives (planning); assemble the necessary resources such as finances, equipment, materials, and human resources (organizing); direct and encourage others to perform the tasks necessary to complete the job (motivating); then check to see that the tasks are being completed according to the plan and make necessary modifications to the plan if needed (controlling).[7]

Planning

"A goal without a plan is just a wish." (Larry Elder)

There is an old saying, if you have no goals, then any path will get you there. Actions without goals result in aimless wandering. As a manager, you must have a good understanding of how your area of responsibility fits into the mission and goals of the organization as well as how these goals affect what you and your subordinates do on a day-to-day basis. Thus, the need for planning.

Simply defined, planning involves the setting of goals and the development of means for achieving those goals.[7] Planning is an essential process in adapting to the constantly changing external environmental influences. Depending upon the organization, planning may be either a formal or informal process. Whether a planning process results in a formal document or a general understanding of a plan's intent, it should be viewed as the organization's marching orders. The plan should not end up in a binder, placed on a shelf, and ignored, but should become a template driving the actions for all managers and employees.

Planning takes place at all levels of the organization though the breadth of planning will vary depending upon the level of the manager. Top level managers will focus on defining the mission and broader goals of the organization. Middle managers will take these broader goals and develop specific objectives and strategies to accomplish them. Lower level managers and supervisors will be assigned the responsibility to see these objectives and strategies are carried out. For example, upper management may set a goal of increasing sales by 10% over the next year; middle managers may then be tasked with developing specific strategies to accomplish this goal, defining the kinds of actions such as promotion efforts, geographic areas to be targeted, and specific sales quotas and approaches to potential customers. Once defined, these strategies are assigned to lower level managers and sales personnel to perform.

Depending upon the organization's participation philosophy, managers at the middle or supervisory levels may or may not be involved in forming these broad goals. If invited, they may be asked to help formulate and/or critique early goal drafts before a final version is adopted. The planning function has two important products: the actual plan and employee understanding and commitment to the plan. Since middle and lower level managers will have responsibility for organizing and executing the plan, having managers and other employees understand the plan and be committed to it is important to its accomplishment. As a manager, you should communicate to your employees how their work contributes to plan accomplishment, helping them understand the importance of their efforts toward organizational success.

There are different time horizons addressed by the planning process: short term and long term goals. Short term goals are to be completed within a one to two year time frame. On the other hand, long term goals have a time horizon of three to five or more years. There is a sharp distinction between short term and long term goals. Long term goals address substantial changes for the organization's future direction. Short term goals address more immediate organization needs. In order to meet long term goals which drive the organization toward its future, there must be a close link between long term goals and short term goals which make it possible to turn the organization toward its desired future.

A frequent planning mistake is to fail to understand the relationship between these time horizons by focusing on short term goals to the detriment of the organization's long range future. For example, if a long range goal is to introduce new products to attract more customers but no efforts are made to develop, test, and deploy such products in the short term, the long term goal will never be realized.

Competent planning involves a thorough assessment of the many factors which influence an organization's growth and development. This involves the assessment of external environmental factors such as economic and market forces, competitive challenges, political and legal constraints, social trends and other critical information which could impact on the organization's ability to survive in that larger environment. Planning also requires a critical assessment of internal environmental capacities and resources needed to meet the goals. If such competent planning is accomplished, the probability of reaching desired goals is greatly enhanced.

The planning process also sets up and provides a framework for accomplishing other management tasks. The planning goals help to define the types of resources and processes needed for the organizing process, impact the communications and directions provided employees which can assist in motivating them, and serve as a control by keeping the organization focused on its main reasons for being while preventing it from spending its resources on distracting opportunities incompatible with its mission. On the other hand, the plan should not serve as a straight jacket, preventing the organization from considering unplanned for opportunities consistent with the organization's mission.

Planning, therefore, is the first step in accomplishing the organization's mission. Without competent planning, the organization risks engaging in disconnected activities which do not address changing customer needs. Ultimately, this can lead to organizational failure. In fact, failure to plan is planning to fail.

Organizing

"Great ideas are not enough, without seeing to the details
they just remain ideas." (Unknown)

The best laid plans are only words on paper until the necessary strategies and actions are developed and executed to make the plan a reality. There are many brilliant plans never realized because they were left on the shelf and ignored.

Thus, organizing activities follow closely after the planning process is completed. Organizing requires an understanding of the goals to be reached and the specification of objectives and strategies to reach the goals; all of which come from the planning process. Organizing requires determination of the varied resources needed to carry out the objectives and strategies including resources such as required time, facilities, equipment, dollars, supplies, human resources, support of stakeholders, and other such resources.

One common factor required of any activity is time. Whether the activity requires only a short time or many months or years, time is basic to any activity or project. For simple activities of short duration, not much time or preparation may be needed. However, projects of longer duration need careful preparation to complete.

Organization requires estimation of the time required to complete the project. Factors which influence time estimation include fixed deadlines, resource ordering and delivery time, time to train employees, set up time, etc. All such factors interact together. For instance, if a customer has a fixed time deadline, it may require more manpower and equipment than if the deadline was more flexible. Once a time estimate has been completed, scheduling the other resources along the time line is possible.

Organization can be thought of as a series of resource streams which come together at various points along the time dimension. Much like an assembly line, supplies, materials, and manpower must be available at the time needed in order to complete the project. Without such sequencing of resources, the project will be difficult to complete on time and on budget. In organizing such a process, intermediate milestones should be set to assess progress and to detect if there are difficulties in reaching the end goal. If there are problems, adjustments to the time line or resources will be needed.

Organizing requires two types of attention: an understanding of the global or broad intentions of the goals and a capacity for attention to detail. For example, knowing your office must move to a new location (the goal) is one thing, but developing the details necessary to make the move is another. Such actions as finding a new location, arranging a lease, setting a moving date, deciding where office equipment will be placed, packing the old office, informing employees and customers of possible disruptions, assigning responsibilities for needed actions, and so forth, must occur in a logical process. Else, when moving day comes, chaos will result. Broad knowledge is needed to organize the sequence of resources to attain the larger goals of the organization or department; however, things get accomplished only if the details get completed.

Most activities or projects involve more than one person and/ or department. These parties have a vested interest in how projects are carried out because implementing these projects will affect how they do their job. These stakeholders must be considered as an activity or project is organized. If not included in the organizing process, they may react to the activity defensively because they legitimately feel the impact of the changes on their work processes or they may resist changes just to resist. It is important to include stakeholders in the initial organizing process in order to assess where changes will affect other individual work flows and to get their commitment to these changes. The extent of their involvement in the organizing process will vary; however, consideration of who will be affected by the proposed activity or project is critical.

As a manager/supervisor, much of your time will be spent organizing and directing the work tasks of your subordinates. This is often a difficult transition, from being the task doer to the task organizer. Since you may have previously done these tasks, there is a strong tendency to step in and do the task yourself rather than organize and direct the tasks for others. In the long run, this behavior will be counterproductive, underutilizing your managerial talents and your subordinates' skills. Your job is to organize and direct the work of others, not do the work which others are capable of doing. Those managers unable or unwilling to delegate tasks are condemned to do everything themselves and increase their likelihood of failure.

Motivating

Managers are supposed to motivate their employees.[7] Motivation is often viewed as something the boss does to the subordinate by carrying a stick in one hand and a carrot in the other. However, this perception is simplistic and does not adequately address the motivation process. Motivation involves both incentives and disincentives provided by the manager and organization as well as understanding and embracing the motivational forces the employee brings to the work place. A basic understanding of how people are motivated is needed by any manager.

In the context of the work place, to motivate is to engage workers in their assigned duties and tasks at a sufficient level of energy and interest to produce the desired outputs. Explanations of motivation are categorized into three broad classifications: need, cognitive, and reinforcement explanations.

Need explanations suggest each person has internal bodily and psychological forces which drive people to behave in ways to meet these needs. These needs vary in intensity and duration depending on how well they are satisfied. Two basic needs are physiological and safety needs.[16] Physiological needs include such fundamental conditions as water, air, nutrition, and livable climatic conditions while safety needs include a reasonably predictable environment, adequate shelter, and a psychological sense of safety and security.

Three social needs or motives are also present: power, achievement, and affiliation.[17] People with power motivation are attracted to tasks and work situations which allow them to exert influence over people and to take responsibility for developing and directing events. Achievement motivated people are attracted to challenging tasks, perform at high levels of achievement, and prefer tasks which stretch their capacities. Affiliation motivated individuals like to work and interact with others, like to work in teams, and like to have close interpersonal relations. These three needs are psychological in nature and, combined with physiological and safety needs, form the basis of our underlying motivation structure.

These needs must find a means of being met through learned behaviors. These behaviors are learned throughout our lives. Whether it is a child learning how to eat and what foods satisfy hunger or an adult learning the skills and actions needed to satisfactorily perform a job, these behaviors serve to meet needs. Behaviors which are successful in fulfilling needs are reinforced and are more likely to be repeated when the needs arise again. Needs are not fixed, unchanged forces but vary depending upon a person's circumstances. For example, if one is hungry, attention to finding food becomes paramount; however, if one has just finished eating, hunger is no longer a strong motivator. Also, needs can vary in strength and thus be experienced with differing levels of intensity. In other words, needs ebb and flow in intensity over time and one's stage of life development.

In addition to learning need fulfillment behaviors through reinforcement, need fulfillment is also assisted through the cognitive/thinking process of goal setting and developing mental strategies for reaching these goals. People set many types of goals related to career, income, employment, recreation, love, friendship, and religion. These goals and strategies provide a type of mental map which indicate the appropriate behaviors needed to meet these goals and the underlying needs these goals address. Goals become motivators in themselves. That is, the goals serve as motivators to direct behavior. For example, if you wish to become a manager, the goal, then you must learn the required knowledge and skills necessary to qualify for the position. Once the required education and experience are obtained, and promotion is given, the goal is reached. Reaching the goal then makes it possible to better meet physiological and safety needs while providing a sense of achievement and a position to exercise power and influence over people and events.

The table below summarizes the above motivational needs and suggests some ideas of how you as manager could meet some of your employees needs.

Table 3: Summary of Motivational Factors

Needs	Definition	Work Place Motivator
Physiological	Fundamental bodily needs such as air, water, food, shelter, etc., for personal survival and growth	Wages, Benefits
Safety	Physical and psychological environments which produce a reasonably secure sense of safety and predictability	Safe work environment, guaranteed employment, predictable wages, supportive colleagues, etc.
Power	A need to control and influence events and people	Positions of responsibility to direct and influence others, organize events, processes, etc.

Achievement	A need to learn, be challenged, and perform excellently	Assigned tasks requiring learning that are challenging and stretch the person's capacities
Affiliation	Need to be with and around other people and interact with them, to have close and meaningful relationships with others	Assigned work space with others, work teams, not isolated, assigned to tasks with people contact
Goal Setting	To set goals and strategies which make it possible to meet one's needs, goals direct behaviors needed to reach the desired ends	Clear work goals and expectations, learning workers' personal and professional goals to assist workers in achieving these goals when possible

All six needs are likely to be active at the same time in differing intensities. Through observation and talking with an employee, you can estimate the importance each need has for the employee and then try as much as possible to arrange the work and work environment to address those needs. Of course, there are limits to how much the work can be arranged to meet individual needs; however, the closer needs can be accommodated, the more motivated the individual is likely to be.

Organizations provide a number of incentives helpful in meeting your employees' needs.[3] Table 4 presents a framework in which to consider these incentives. Organizational incentives involve rule enforcement, economic incentives, and internal motives.

Table 4: Organizational Motivational Patterns

Rule Enforcement	Economic Incentives	Internal Motives

• Use of Power
• Use of Authority
• Policy/ Procedure Manuals
• External Signs of Authority
• Legal Compliance
• Supervision
• Formal Control Systems
	• Pay/Compensation
	• Fringe Benefits
	• Bonuses
	• Profit Sharing
	• Praise
	• Recognition
	• Pleasant Working Conditions
	• Job Security
		• Encourage Learning/ Acceptance of Organizational Values and Goals
		• Promote Understanding of Product/Service
		• Demonstrate Value of Organization to Community and Society
		• Encourage Self-Identification/ Expression
		  • Intrinsic Job Satisfaction
		  • Responsibility
		  • Personal Sense of Accomplishment
		  • Job Enlargement/ Enrichment
		• Promote Group Belongingness
		  • Shared Sense of Task Accomplishment
		  • Professional Identification
		  • Technical/Craftsman Identification
		  • Social Enrichment

Rule enforcement involves defined regulations, procedures, and expectations which communicate what is expected of employees. Such rules are communicated through a variety of means such as employee handbooks, procedure manuals, and other formal and informal modes. Two extremes must be avoided: too many and too few rules. Too many rules lead to a burdensome bureaucratic environment which can stifle creativity and initiative. Too few rules can lead to lack of direction, ill defined expectations, and undisciplined employee behaviors. Rules provide a way of communicating desired behaviors and maintain a reasonably predictable and safe working environment.

Economic incentives provide the means of supporting the necessary monetary needs to meet the demands of survival and the extras of life. They include such incentives as wages, bonuses, and benefits of various types as listed in the table above. All employees need to work to meet their individual and family survival needs and economic incentives address these needs.

Employees come to the work place with internal motives which can be helpful to the manager. These internal motives include such examples as the employee's interest in the job, personal achievement, power and affiliation needs, career aspirations, pride in one's work, craft and professional identification, and more. In fact, internal motivations are the most powerful motivations once basic economic needs are met.

The above table suggests people are motivated by both external and internal incentives. External motivators are offered by the organization such as wages, while internal motivators are formed by the internal motivational and cognitive processes of the individual. Motivating employees requires an understanding that people have their own individual motive pattern of needs and goals. Many managers fail to recognize the variety of motive patterns and try to motivate everyone in the same manner. An example is the frequently made assumption that money is the sole reason why people work. Certainly money is one of the primary reasons. Money is especially important to those not earning enough to meet basic physiological and safety needs. However, once earning enough to meet these needs, other motives may become more effective in engaging employees in attaining desired goals. Many studies of incentives suggest that money is ranked third or fourth in importance compared to such incentives as self improvement, challenging work, and opportunity for advancement.

There are two strategies for motivating employees which should be practiced by every manager. You should praise and thank your workers for a job well done; that is, frequently reward the behavior you want in order to get people to continue that behavior.[18] The other strategy is to not only approach your workers when you have a problem but to also be around when things are going well. If the only time an employee encounters you is when there is a problem, it will not take many such contacts before the employee hides from you. You should make a practice of frequently taking time to positively interact with employees on a regular basis so as not to become a negative reinforcement. Many managers practice "Management by walking around." This involves just leisurely moving about the department, greeting employees, talking about family and other social topics, asking how the employees work might be assisted, and just being available to listen to employees. Not only is a more relaxed work environment produced but workers become more open and comfortable with the boss and the manager gets a better sense of the work place.

Of all the responsibilities managers face, learning what motivates employees may be the most challenging. Hopefully, the above basic motivation concepts will help you in becoming a successful motivator.

Controlling

> *"Control is a two edged sword, without enough of it chaos will reign, with too much of it stagnation and/or rebellion results."* (Unknown)

For many people, control is a dirty word, conjuring up images of oppressive restrictions which prevent personal freedom and spontaneity. Yet without control in the work place, little would get accomplished. In general, controlling serves to regulate activities so that the products or services of the organization are produced according to plan.[7]

In order to get people and other resources to focus on the activities needed to accomplish tasks, it is necessary for you to establish and enforce expectations of behaviors of employees to complete the work of the organization. The means by which this control is exerted are many. In performing the managerial processes of planning, organizing, and motivating, many of the control processes are developed. For example, the planned goals provide direction. Organizing assembles and develops the specific tasks and resources needed to meet the goals, while motivating encourages employees to carry out the tasks needed to reach the goals. Another aspect of controlling is frequently checking to see that critical tasks are completed as planned. If not occurring according to plan, corrective action is needed to get back on plan or the plan is modified to fit unexpected deviations.

Many specific methods are used by managers to control employees and the tasks they do to meet the necessities of organizational performance. Three levels of controls are evident: organizational, group, and individual. Organization level controls tend to be system wide or systemic. For example, employee handbooks specify rules and regulations for all employees ranging from expected start and stop times for work, vacation policies, personal and sick days, dress codes, safety rules, and so forth. At the group level (division, department, work groups, informal groups), controls include examples such as production quotas, performance and quality standards, group values, and professional and ethical standards. Individual level controls include such things as salary and wages, fringe benefits, individual performance goals, and promotion and advancement. Controlling not only acts as a means of insuring compliance with organization needs but can also act as incentives for employees, as discussed in the section on motivation.

In addition to the internal controls discussed above, many external forces control or influence organizational behavior. Federal, state, and local government regulations provide legal and political restraints. Accreditation agencies set and enforce expected standards (International Organization for Standardization [ISO], the Joint Hospital Commission, academic regional accreditation associations, professional associations, financial reporting requirements, etc.). These and many other external controls influence what an organization and its employees can and cannot do.

Controls direct and restrain behaviors. They are necessary to provide structure and coherence for the workforce to complete the organization's work. Two dangers are always present. Too many or unnecessary controls lead to suffocating bureaucracy while not enough directions and controls lead to confusion and great inefficiency. Thus, finding the right balance between controls and flexibility is the constant challenge of managers. As a manager/ supervisor, a significant portion of your efforts will be spent in such activities. Making sure the work of your subordinates is accomplished according to plan, meeting quality standards, and performing in time and on budget requires you to be both enforcer and motivator, parent and friend, task definer and relationship builder, a daunting responsibility.

Managing Meetings

As a manager, a good part of your time will be taken up with group meetings. Whether it be a meeting with a work team, department, or committee, you will need some familiarity with group functioning and how to run a meeting. Whether as leader or participant, knowledge of how groups function will make your meetings more productive.

Unfortunately, much time and expense is wasted in meetings. For example, a group of ten people meeting for one hour represents 10 man hours. If this time is not well structured and facilitated, the meeting can waste much time and expense. Time spent in nonproductive meetings can be enormously frustrating to participants as little is accomplished and talent is wasted. For this and other reasons, knowing how groups work and how the leader and other participants should conduct themselves is critical.

Types of Meetings. Meetings are held for one of three reasons: information sharing, discussion of issues, and/or decision making. An information dissemination meeting contains only the presentation of information to participants and involves little comment or discussion of the presented material. A topic discussion meeting involves concentration on topics which require sharing of ideas, developing potential solutions to problems, policy formation, and formulating recommendations. Decision making meetings decide upon selecting and approving/recommending actions based upon previous thorough discussions of topics. From this type of meeting, final decisions are made for implementation. Meetings can be single purpose, e.g., to disseminate information or a combination of these three reasons. Mixtures of these meeting types within the same meeting are common.

Impediments to Successful Meetings. There are three major impediments to successful and productive meetings: lack of proper structuring and timing of an agenda, lack of participant preparation, and poor meeting facilitation. Agenda building preparation prior to a meeting is the first step to a successful meeting. Whatever the meeting purpose, several basic actions are needed to structure the meeting.

- An agenda must be developed by determining the list of topics to be addressed. This can be done by listing topics contributed by both leader and participants.

- Ordering these items by importance and criticalness and then assigning them to an appropriate place on the agenda comes next. Since the list may take longer then the allotted time for the meeting, it is important that the more pressing items be addressed first with lower priority items left to future meetings.

- It is then wise to estimate the amount of time to be allotted to each item and affix start and ending times to indicate how much time each item is to be discussed. Providing time parameters for discussion helps structure participant focus and prevent discussions from wandering off on unrelated topics. Specific time allotments make it possible to complete all agenda items in the time limits of the meeting. If discussion of a specific item requires more time than allotted, the leader/participants can decide whether the discussion should continue in this meeting or be postponed until another time. If it is decided to continue in the meeting, a decision to move later items on the agenda to another meeting can be made.

- The agenda should also indicate who is responsible for presenting each agenda item, and what preparation on the part of participants is needed prior to the meeting.

- All participants should receive a copy of the agenda prior to the meeting.

Participant preparation is critical to an effective meeting. Those responsible for specific agenda items must come prepared to present the topic, including copies of needed documents for group members. If other participants should have reviewed documents prior to the meeting, these documents should be distributed in ample time prior to the meeting.

Facilitation of meetings involves arranging for appropriate physical, material, and equipment needs, and conducting the meeting to maximize accomplishment of its goals as represented by the agenda. Depending upon the needs of the group, the proper physical environment for the meeting must be arranged and essential materials and equipment should be provided, along with any other physical needs which will support the smooth functioning of the group. There is nothing more frustrating than to need resources but not have them available. This can disrupt the productivity of the group and cause unneeded interruption and delay in accomplishing meeting objectives.

Conducting the actual meeting requires at least one person to facilitate the meeting. The formal leader of the group could be the facilitator or another member could be assigned this role. This person's role is to focus on the group process, ideally not taking part in the actual discussion/problem solving but guiding the members through the process. The facilitator must be aware of two components of group functioning: content and member behavior. Content, or task, refers to the actual meeting material discussed and produced by the participants. This includes the specific ideas, points of view, and opinions expressed by group members. Member behavior refers to vocal intonations of members and their non-verbal behaviors which reveal their attention levels, readiness to express ideas, emotional involvement, and engagement with the group. Attention to these two components of group functioning, content and member behavior, is critical to effective group facilitation. These components assist group members to focus on exploring each topic, not wander into unrelated or tangential issues, while insuring each person has opportunities to contribute and be involved in the discussion as appropriate.

There are a number of specific behaviors which you should learn in order to be a competent facilitator and group member. Two types of behaviors need mastering: task and group maintenance/building functions.[19] Task functions address behaviors helpful in keeping the group focused on the goals and tasks of the group. These roles/behaviors are presented in the table below.

Table 5: Task Functions

Task Role	Role Behavior
Idea Generator	Presents ideas, suggestions, novel approaches, solutions and decisions, etc.
Information Seeker/ Giver	Asks for or gives idea clarification, information or facts relevant to group discussion
Opinion Seeker/ Giver	Asks for group members' opinions and feelings about the task; states own opinions about other members' ideas, attitudes, and contributions
Elaborator	Clarifies ideas and contributions, explains underlying assumptions of ideas, hypothesizes how suggestions will impact the organization
Coordinator	Draws out interrelationships among ideas, suggestions, and facts; tries to integrate them into a coherent whole
Diagnostician	Identifies what the task issues and problems are
Orientor	Keeps the group focused on the goals, tasks, and summarizes group interactions
Energizer	Motivates members to keep working on the goals and tasks of the group
Evaluator	Assesses group progress and whether members have reached agreement

Group maintenance/building functions address behaviors needed to help the group build cohesiveness, morale, and communications. These roles/behaviors are presented in the table below.

Table 6: Group Maintenance/Building Functions

Group Maintenance Roles	Group Maintenance Behaviors
Supporter	Positively reinforces the efforts and contributions of group members; provides a warm, comfortable, and accepting environment
Harmonizer	Encourages members to explore differences of opinion, helps to find common ground by reconciling differences
Tension Reliever	Reduces tense situations through humor, irreverent comments, observations of group incongruities, etc.
Compromiser	Willing to compromise with those who hold differing opinions, works to produce harmony in the group
Gatekeeper	Builds member interactions by keeping communication channels open
Feeling Expresser	Reveals and shares emotions, feelings, and relationships of self and other group members
Standard Setter	Sets and evaluates the goals and standards to be met by group members
Follower	Follows the lead of other group members by passively listening and accepting their ideas and opinions

Learning to appropriately use the behaviors of task and group maintenance/building functions will help groups perform productively. However, not all member behaviors are helpful. Some behaviors reflect individual needs which may be counter to and dysfunctional for the goals of the group. Eight such disruptive behaviors are presented in the table below.[19]

Table 7: Group Disruptive Behaviors

Dysfunctional Roles	Behavior Description
Blocker	Interferes with group progress by continually disagreeing and stopping others from expressing ideas and refusing to cooperate with members
Aggressor	Attempts to raise own status by belittling others, by bragging, and by criticizing others
Deserter	Stays withdrawn, aloof and above it all; acts with excessive formality, engages in joking, side conversations, and distracts other members
Dominator	Attempts to take over the group by monopolizing the conversation, speaking continually, and interrupting other members
Recognition Seeker	Seeks attention and sympathy by boasting of accomplishments and introducing unrelated personal experiences
Confessor	Uses the group to express unrelated personal limitations and feelings
Comedian	Uses inappropriate humor, behavior, and cynicism to remain uninvolved with the group
Special Interest Pleader	Presents self as representing and advocating for some other group, individual, or cause not related to the group's purpose

Poorly designed and executed meetings which lack focus, goal clarity, and effective facilitation can result in wasted manpower and time, leading to poor decision making, immense frustration, and lowered productivity and morale.

Meetings are inevitable in any organization. They are one of the means by which communication, discussion of issues, problem solving, and decision making occur. They are a means of bringing the collective brains and experience of any organization to bear on important issues and decisions. An effective manager must seek the knowledge and training required to be a strong facilitator and a productive participant in all meetings.

Processes

One of the most important responsibilities of a manager is developing, implementing, and maintaining processes and their supportive standards and procedures. Every department/unit in an organization has assigned tasks which must be completed in order to keep the organization's work flow and outputs predictable, efficient, and cost effective. It is your job as manager to supervise these processes.

All processes have components: output goals, standards, procedures, and hardware and software technologies, employees with the appropriate knowledge and skills, and appropriate training for workers. The nature of each task determines the specific characteristics of each of these components. As a manager, you must educate yourself about each of these processes, understand how they contribute to the workflow of the department/unit, and evaluate their effectiveness in contributing to the department's and organization's goals.

Managers must realize that department processes are often interdependent. Changes in or problems with one task process may create difficulties with other processes. Therefore, learning these interdependencies is critical to the performance of the department. Further, it is very likely that the performance of departmental processes impacts the work of other departments. Generally, the outputs of one department serve as work inputs for other departments. Thus, the interconnectedness of these processes must be well understood by the manager. Changes in the processes of one department can have consequences for other departments. Therefore, the manager who would change department processes must be aware of how these changes could create difficulties/ changes in other departments and their work flow.

For example, procurement may decide to purchase a less costly material with slightly different qualities which in turn causes difficulties in the manufacturing procedures because it means adjusting these procedures to accommodate the changed characteristics of the material. Another example is a hospital pharmacy which changes its drug distribution system but fails to inform the ward nurses of this change. The failure to communicate this change, in turn, causes disruption of ward routine and mistakes in medicating patients.

Managers try to develop processes which are efficient, cost effective, and well suited to the stable and smooth functioning of the department. However, nothing remains the same forever. New demands on the organization occur; customers want changes in the product/service; new technologies emerge which improve on past processes; employees come up with ideas of how to improve what they do; and so forth. As a manager, you must be ever alert to these changing conditions and be willing to alter the established processes as appropriate to the situation. This means constant assessment of processes to see how they can be improved. Change for change sake is not good but resistance to needed change can be a death knoll to the organization. You should be always looking for means of reducing cost while keeping quality of products/services at acceptable levels. The goal of continuous improvement[20] should be an on-going philosophy. It argues that all processes must be constantly improved to squeeze out unnecessary actions and costs. No process ever reaches the point that it can remain the same forever.

Case Study: Dean of Academic Administration

As Dean of Academic Administration, Ed was faced with an interesting student request. The student wanted to divide up credit hours earned for one purpose into fractions of hours (2.4, 1.5, etc.) and apply these credits to other graduation requirements. Clearly the student was trying to make her advancement to her degree easier and trying to avoid taking courses she would prefer not to take. Still the request raised an interesting point: should fractions of credit hours be allowed to apply to areas not generally permitted? As interpreter of academic policy, allowing such fractionalization of credit would surely open up the flood gates for other such requests if allowed. Ed decided the intent of the faculty in legislating academic policy did not include this option and he denied the request.

Ed managed several areas including student registration and records, enforcing academic regulations, and a 5 million dollar academic budget encompassing 23 majors. He directed the administrative computer support staff, the development of the College Bulletin, academic calendar development, and assembling governmental reports, to name a few responsibilities. His direct reports included six registrarial personnel and institutional research. He maintained a close working relationship with the accounting and the financial aid offices. Ed also worked with each academic department chair to review and monitor budgets to insure approved dollar amounts were not exceeded during the fiscal year.

Since student registrations formed the basis of tuition revenue and affect student financial aid balances, the registration process had to be convenient for students but also accurate and timely. To underscore the registration process importance, a recent problem had emerged, called the "accounts receivable" problem. Some students were receiving bills for classes they had dropped, thus causing problems with unhappy students, angry parents over inflated income projections for the college, and internal tensions between the affected offices. Ed was chairing a meeting that morning to identify the causes of the problem. This meant reviewing registration processes, how this information was processed by the computer, how the information was transferred to the business and financial aid offices, and then correcting the appropriate processes.

As it turned out, it took more than one meeting to identify several causes, including difficulties with the registration staff in understanding how to enter course information into the computer and a glitch in the computer software in communicating information to each student's account which, in turn, was charging the financial aid balance of the student. Thus, Ed found himself acting as meeting facilitator, conflict resolver, and problem solver. To correct the errant processes required developing a better training process for registrarial personnel and working with computer and business staff to modify the software to provide the correct information. Additionally, Ed was also tasked with contacting each student and the student's parents to explain the reasons for the problem, smoothing ruffled feathers, and communicating what steps were being taken to correct the problem.

The centrality of the registrarial process to the functioning of the college was underscored by this incident. The basic class enrollment information interacts with other college processes. Not only was the billing process impacted but also the lives of students, their families, faculty, and the overall functioning and financial health of the institution.

Budgeting

> *"Eventually, a manager will have to say 'No' to everyone*
> *and no one likes to hear 'No.'"* (Unknown)

When you are promoted to management, it is very likely you will be involved in your unit's budgeting process. Budgeting serves both the planning and control management processes and is primarily the responsibility of the organization's system of managers, though members of the other systems within the organization may also be involved. In its planning role, budgeting helps determine the income and expenses associated with both long and short term goals set through the planning process. In its control role, the budget is used to monitor how projected income and expenses as contained in the budget are tracking with the plan. If more money is being spent than forecasted, adjustments to the plan can be made before the spending gets out of hand.

Budgeting is based upon the accounting system's Chart of Accounts developed by the financial officers. This Chart defines the subaccounts needed to track all financial transactions. The Chart not only addresses internal reporting needs but also addresses external reporting such as those required to meet professional accounting standards; federal, state, and local taxes; investor reports; and the needs of other institutions to which the organization's financial health must be communicated.

Within each department, specific subaccounts are defined which categorize the major income and expense activities of the department. Common accounts include salary and wages, supplies, telephone, contractor expense, equipment, and so forth. The specific activities of each department may require accounts unique to the department.

Budgets are formed based upon the fiscal year (FY). The most frequently used FYs are January 1 to December 31 or July 1 to June 30. The fiscal year is assigned the year in which the budget begins, e.g., FY12, FY13, etc. The accounts assigned to each department are used to develop the departmental budget. The most common budget development model is the previous budget plus or minus next year's estimates. Other budget models are used less often, such as zero based budgeting or top down budgeting where higher level managers award a certain total budget dollar amount which the department must live within.

The first model requires looking at past experience and then estimating whether an increase or decrease is needed for the next year. To make a budget estimate, assumptions about inflation rates, increases, or decreases in activities related to planning goals must be made. Once all these factors are considered, each account amount is added to all other account amounts to form the departmental budget. The totals from all other departments are accumulated to form the organization's budget for the fiscal year.

A close integration of planning goals with the budget is critical because the budget sets the financial expectations for the organization. Budgets must be honest estimates of expected income and expenses. Budgeting can become a playground for fiscal game playing. One such game is a tendency for departments to overestimate expenses and underestimate income. If done throughout the organization, this will result in an unrealistic budget long in expenses and short in income or, put another way, a deficit budget. On the other hand, top level managers have a tendency to overestimate income and force these overestimates upon income producing departments. Such budgeting maneuvers can only lead to flawed budget projections and future problems.

Case Study: Restaurateur

At 3:35am, Judy's bedside phone rang with a message from the security company that an alarm had just gone off at the restaurant. The police were on the way and she should meet them at the site ASAP. Upon arriving at the restaurant, she found the police officers inspecting a hole in the front plate glass window apparently caused by someone who was drunk falling into it. Some blood on the window ledge and in the snow suggested the culprit did not walk away unscathed. The police escorted Judy through the restaurant looking for intruders. Fortunately, none were found. Now she would have to wait in the freezing restaurant until the glass company arrived, probably not before customers arrived at 6:30am. Well, this was not the way she wanted to begin her day but her day had started anyway.

Judy was Director of Operations (DO) responsible for three restaurants which were part of a larger chain of eateries. Each restaurant had a General Manager (GM) whom she supervised and worked closely with on a daily basis. In fact, she was also temporarily serving as the GM for one of the sites while a new GM was being sought. Thus, she not only rotated among the three sites but she had daily duties at one of them.

Judy's responsibilities were many. She was responsible for the income, cost control, and profitability of each restaurant; hiring and training of personnel; food and beverage ordering; equipment purchasing and repair; developing systems for food and beverage portion control; assuring health department regulations were met or exceeded; scheduling employees, facility maintenance and cleaning; assuring that ticket times (time from customer order to food delivery) were maintained at acceptable levels; menu planning; publicity and promotion; and reporting to corporate headquarters all aspects of the operations.

One challenge for Judy was keeping employees motivated. Keeping them happy and focused on their job was a constant demand. Judy kept in touch with each person on a regular basis, providing a structured training for new employees, checking to see that her GMs were following through on their responsibilities, asking employees about how the work environment could be improved, trying to meet their work schedule needs in the best way possible, soliciting ideas about improving customer service and menu improvements, challenging cooks to try new food specials, trialing customer suggestions for food items, and generally creating a friendly, supportive work environment for all employees.

Guest relations were another important priority for Judy and her GMs and other employees. If the guests were unhappy, the restaurant would fail. In addition to having pleasant and competent serving staff who relate well to customers, Judy and the GMs visited each table, asking about guest satisfaction with service, quality of food, and any suggestions they had for improvements. Such visits gave Judy a chance to get a sense of guest contentment and to respond to complaints and/or suggestions.

Her biggest challenge was maintaining profitability. Judy developed a system by which she was able to track profitability on a daily/hourly basis. She was able to query her data base about all costs, including income, personnel costs, food costs, and all fixed costs to assess hour by hour profitability. This gave her a comparison to the same day one year ago and allowed her and her GMs to make informed decisions about the number of cooks/ servers needed at any given time. This information was critical in maintaining cost, profit, and budget control. One of her biggest difficulties was equipment failure, especially cooking/kitchen equipment. Breakdown of this equipment led to large repair and/ or purchasing costs which were difficult to anticipate and had a dramatic impact on decreasing profitability.

As important as her job of DO was, it had its less glamorous side. Yes, she was the chief manager for the three restaurants; however, she also must be able and willing to perform every job in the restaurant. If the restaurant gets "slammed," Judy may end up cooking, waiting tables, bussing tables, expediting food orders, and even washing dishes. In fact, she warned anyone thinking about going into the restaurant business that they must be willing to put in long hours and do any job necessary to make a success of the business.

Evaluation

Everyone gets evaluated. Whether this happens by design or by happenstance, formally or informally, we all get evaluated. Why evaluation? Because to survive, all organizations must perform at least at a minimally productive level in order to meet the demands of their customers and the broader expectations of society.

Evaluation takes place at many levels such as corporate wide assessment of financial performance, quality control of products or services, performance measures in markets, value assessment to society, etc. Division and department evaluations are a must to assess how well these subunits perform and contribute to the organization. Processes within these units are evaluated to assess how efficiently and effectively they operate. However, all of the above levels of evaluation ultimately come down to how well individual people are performing their jobs. The collective efforts of all employees determine how well an organization succeeds.

When you accept a supervisor or manager role it will surely require you to become an evaluator of your subordinates. Personnel evaluation systems typically include two main categories: task and personal characteristics. Task characteristics involve assessing the employee's intellectual capacities, skills, and overall ability to accomplish the tasks/job responsibilities. Personal characteristics involve assessing the employee's ability to communicate with and relate to others, commitment to the job, motivation level, punctuality, honesty, and so forth. Together, these task and personal characteristics are rated/judged in reference to the job requirements and contribution to the organization.

Many methods of employee evaluation are used. Some organizations regularly review employee performance while others have informal processes. Formal systems usually involve simple rating scales including traits such as dependability, accuracy, timeliness, etc. Others may have formal objectives each employee must achieve (management by objectives, MBO). Another evaluation process is called 360 degree evaluations where not only the manager evaluates the employee but so do his/her peers and other people who depend upon the employee's performance. Still other organizations may rely on informal processes where the manager simply observes the employee and decides if the person is doing an acceptable job. Whatever the approach, you, as manager, play a central role in the evaluation process.

The consequences of failing to assess employee job performance are many. Allowing poor performance to continue can undermine an organization's ability to survive. It can result in poor products or service to customers. It can result in inadequate support to departments, divisions, and processes throughout the organization. Since workers generally know how fellow workers are performing, letting a poor performer continue without corrective actions often results in demoralizing other employees and consequent decline in their own performance. Additionally, failure to recognize and reward exceptional performance and tolerating laggards send a message to the entire workforce that excellent performance is not valued and poor performance is acceptable. Such acceptance of mediocrity or worse can lead to unacceptable performance at best and organizational failure at worst.

Many managers do not like to evaluate employees because of the tension it raises between themselves and the employee.

However, this is not an adequate excuse to avoid performance reviews. To avoid this duty is to fail in one's responsibilities.

A well designed evaluation system should give employees feedback on both their strengths and areas of needed improvement, a time line for improving deficiencies, and suggestions for achievement of these improvements. It is not enough to simply indicate that improvement is needed. The manager/organization should provide help to improve worker weaknesses such as additional training, workshops, educational opportunities, and skill training, as appropriate. If subsequent evaluations find the employee either unable and/or unwilling to improve these weaknesses, then dismissal must be considered.

Regular performance reviews carry other implications for the individual and the organization. Documentation of individual performance over time is important for rewarding and recognizing employee development, mastering skills and knowledge, future promotions, pay increases, and overall recognition of employee contributions. Records of this history are important for subsequent managers. There are also legal requirements for employment history especially if it becomes necessary to consider termination of employment.

Evaluation is necessary for the survival of any organization. Evaluation is part of both the controlling and motivating processes of management. Without good and consistent evaluation processes, excellent organizational performance over time will be in jeopardy.

Hiring and Dismissal

Two of the most important processes managers are responsible for are hiring and firing/dismissal of employees. These two processes involve great expenditures of time and dollars. Hiring done well contributes to the overall productivity of the organization. Hiring done poorly leads to enormous expenditures of time and dollars, employee dissatisfaction, and eventually dismissal.

For example, hiring an engineer who performed poorly was found to cost the firm approximately $350,000 including such expenditures as initial recruiting costs, pre employment interviewing and testing, training, two years compensation and wages, loss of effective engineering contributions, and severance costs. From the poorly hired person's point of view, being hired into a job for which he/she is inappropriate can lead to devastating personal failure and a permanent black mark on his/her career and work record.

Dismissal done well rids the organization of unproductive employees and the wasted dollars and poor productivity associated with them. Dismissal done poorly can lead to unnecessary personal injury to the dismissed employee, expensive litigation, and negative impact on the remaining employees' morale and the organization's reputation for fairness and ethical standards.

Hiring. Hiring should be one of the enjoyable functions for a manager. It provides an opportunity to select a person who can contribute to the overall needs of the organization as well as make the manager's job easier. However, some managers see the hiring process as interfering with their busy schedule, and take little interest in preparing for the effort needed to do it well. This is unfortunate since hiring a qualified person should lead to better departmental productivity as well as being a benefit to the manager. Though hiring does take time, the time spent to hire a good employee takes infinitely less time than hiring a poorly performing person and then having to dismiss the person later.

There are a number of steps in the hiring process. However, depending on the size of the organization, the level of the employee being hired, and other factors, how involved a manager might be in each step varies widely. In a small organization the manager might be involved in every step, while in larger organizations these steps may be administered by human resource personnel, leaving the manager minimal time involvement.

The following steps are involved in the hiring process:

- Developing/modifying the position's job description;

- Determining the appropriate education, training, skills, experience, and personality characteristics needed for the job;

- Determining salary/wage and benefits level for the job;

- Recruiting candidates from both internal posting and external advertising;

- Reviewing applications and resumes;

- Selecting the most qualified candidates for further assessment;

- Ability, skill, and personality testing as appropriate;

- Interviewing the candidates;

- Selecting the most qualified person;

- Offering the job and negotiating the compensation package; and

- Informing those candidates who were not chosen of the decision.

Dismissal. One of the most difficult situations you may face is dismissing an employee. Dismissing an employee represents a failure on the part of the employee either to meet the standards of the organization and/or to meet the requirements of the job. Dismissing an employee may also be a failure on the part of the organization either for hiring the wrong person for the job to begin with, failing to provide the necessary support to the individual for meeting the requirements of the job, or not being prepared for changing economic conditions. There are a number of reasons for these failures. These reasons include:

- The inability or unwillingness of the employee to meet performance expectations,

- Poor employee training and support to assist employees to improve knowledge and skills necessary for changing job requirements,

- The evolution of the original job which now exceeds the employee's capacity,

- Organizational change resulting in the elimination of the job, and

- Economic conditions within or external to the organization forcing downsizing of the workforce.

Dismissal, therefore, can result not only because of employee limitations but also relate to organizational conditions not conducive to job continuation.

In general, dismissal involves one of two major reasons: for cause or changing organizational conditions. Dismissal for cause/ poor employee performance includes the following procedures/ steps:

- Assemble documentation from previous evaluations supporting the dismissal;

- Involve higher level officials in reviewing reasons for dismissal and consistency with organizational policies;

- Get approval to proceed;

- Hold dismissal interview with employee, provide reasons for dismissal;

- Give information on severance package, outplacement services, insurance information, and name of contact person for further questions;

- Provide date of last day of work or immediate removal from work site; and

- Secure vital information sources held by individual: computers, files, documents, etc.

Dismissing employees because of organizational needs is very different from dismissing for cause. Layoffs or reductions in force (RIF) are painful to both the involved employees and the organization itself. These actions result in the loss of valuable employees and the loss of expertise, talent, and human resources needed to keep the organization running at previous levels. Though many of the procedures mentioned above for cause dismissal are the same for RIFs, RIF dismissals are much more devastating to the entire company. In informing employees of their layoff, it is important to communicate to them their release is not their fault, that their contributions to the organization are appreciated, and that their presence will be missed. Surely, they will not be happy at their dismissal but should be treated as fairly as possible. Depending upon organizational resources, efforts should be made to help make the employee departure as easy as possible.

Many of the steps listed above for cause and RIF dismissals require experience and knowledge, and may require the manager to seek help and advice from other organizational authorities.

For both hiring and dismissal, the one skill that you must develop is interviewing. Whether you are interviewing to fill an open position or conducting a dismissal interview, developing interviewing skills is a must. There are many books, training videos, and training seminars available to develop these skills and these resources should be utilized by managers.

The Organization

"Win/Win can only survive in an organization when the systems support it. If you talk Win/Win but reward Win/Lose, you've got a losing program on your hands."

Stephen R. Covey

Organizational Design

Managers do not operate in a vacuum; rather, they function within the boundaries of an organization. Management's purpose for being is the accomplishment of the mission and goals of the organization. Understanding your position in relationship to the larger organization, the functions your position serves, and your place within the governance structure is important to your success as well as that of the organization.

All organizations are social systems composed of people gathered together to accomplish a common purpose. To do this, various resources are needed such as physical facilities, equipment, money, technologies, and energy. However, without the proper people accomplishing appropriate tasks, the organization will fail.

Generic Functions. All organizations share common elements called generic functions. These basic functions are performed by specific groups, departments, managers/supervisors, and employees gathered into subgroups/subsystems. These basic functions are the fundamental elements underlying all organizations whatever their size.[3] These basic functions include:

- Productive functions,

- Supportive functions,

- Adaptive functions,

- Maintenance functions, and the

- Managerial function.

Each manager plays a role in at least one of the first four functions as performed through its subsystem, as well as participating in the managerial function by being a member of its subsystem. As each subsystem is described, you should identify which one(s) your position serves.

Productive Subsystems. Productive subsystems include those organizational elements responsible for processing or making the products and services for which the organization was founded. For example, automobile manufacturers assemble cars; educational institutions educate students; hospitals treat illness and produce healthier people; and financial institutions produce investment income. Productive subsystems are considered the primary organizational subsystems because without them the organization would have nothing to sell and, thus, no way to produce income to support the remaining generic functions.

The importance of the productive subsystems is illustrated by a laundry company vigorously promoting its services to increase its customer base despite warnings its productive subsystems (washing, drying, sorting, ironing, mending) would be unable to deal with the increased business. The promotion succeeded but the increased demands on the antiquated and poorly maintained equipment resulted in poor performance, losing both new and old customers and, eventually, closing the business itself.

The four remaining generic functions support the activities of the productive subsystems.

Supportive Subsystems. Supportive subsystems directly connect to the productive subsystems and either provide needed resources used in the production process or assist in disposing of the finished product or service to customers. Recruiting students for a school, purchasing raw materials needed in manufacturing a product, advertising to attract customers to eat in a restaurant, selling merchandise in a department store, delivering already purchased merchandise to a buyer are examples of procurement/ disposal activities. The processes of procuring resources or disposing of product are boundary spanning activities, interacting with the organization's internal and external environments. In this manner, the organization maintains needed inputs from the external environment (its vendors, customers/markets) and disposes of (sells) its products or services. This produces income which in turn acts as an input from the environment.

This is a cyclical process essential to the continued well being of the organization. Without this continued input from the environment, the production of goods or services, and the selling of them, the organization would cease to exist. Because of this continual interacting, supportive subsystems are change oriented as they attempt to meet external demands and bring these demands into the organization.

Adaptive Subsystems. Adaptive subsystems are concerned with assessing the external environment. These subsystems are focused on detecting changing circumstances to which the organization must adapt in order to continue functioning. Adaptive subsystems include such functions as product development, market research, competition analysis, economic forecasting, analysis of customer trends, and other intelligence related to the functioning of the organization.

Because of this orientation to the external environment, adaptive subsystems, similar to supportive subsystems as described above, are also change oriented, alerting the organization to environmental changes which must be accommodated if the organization is to remain vital. Failure to heed changes in customer needs/desires brings to mind Henry Ford's famous remark, "They can have any color car they like, as long as it is black." This attitude led to a sharp decline in Ford sales and provided an entry point for his competitors to grab a large market share from Ford.

Maintenance Subsystems. Maintenance subsystems are focused on the development and maintaining of the essential infrastructure of the organization. Such functions as accounting, budgeting, human resources, information systems, security, buildings and grounds are examples of these subsystems. Often, customers and employees are relatively unaware of the presence of these functions until a water pipe breaks, the temperature of buildings becomes uncomfortable, electrical service fails, parking lot potholes gobble up cars, payroll checks are late, needed employees go unhired, and so forth. Though not directly involved in the productive processes, these subsystems are critical to maintaining a stable and predictable internal working environment. Once this stable working climate has been established, these subsystems tend to resist changes which threaten this stability.

Managerial Subsystem. When you accept a managerial/ supervisory position, you become a member of this subsystem. The managerial subsystem is present in the other four generic subsystems. That is, each of these subsystems has managers who guide those subsystems. The managerial subsystem has as its focus the direction, control, and coordination of all the organization's activities. Managers plan and give direction; they solve conflicts and resolve differences between other subsystems; and they bind organizational elements together so that all components of the organization pull together in the same direction. Without the managerial subsystem, this integration of direction would not likely occur since the other generic subsystems have a strong tendency to pursue their own interests, ignoring the overarching needs of the organization's mission and goals.

Thus, as a manager, you have your feet in two worlds and serve two masters, responsible for the direction and well being of a specific function and at the same time responsible for integrating that function with the organization's global needs. It is the rare manager who has not experienced the pull between the need for additional resources only to find the needs of other parts of the organization trump his/her departmental needs.

Governance Structure. The familiar organizational chart (Figure 1) defines the formal reporting and communication structures of the managerial subsystem.

Figure 1: Organizational Chart

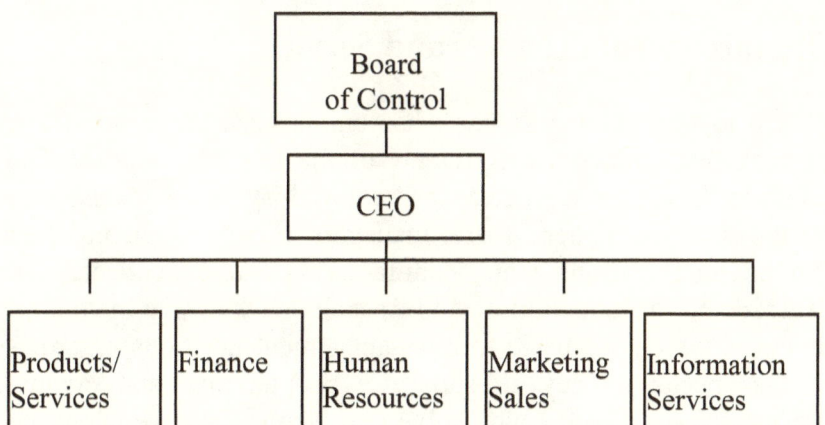

This structure also outlines the governance system which includes two major elements: the executive functions and the administrative functions. The executive functions relate to the policy formation and decision making authority of the organization. This authority typically rests with the Board of Control, the Chief Executive Officer (CEO), and the vice presidential level. Depending upon the organization's governance philosophy, lower level managers and employees may have a role in decision and policy making as practiced in participative management programs. Administrative functions include the day to day management of the organization in which the direction and policies developed by the executive functions are carried out at all levels of the managerial subsystem. Most new managers begin their responsibilities at the administrative level. Since managers come from the various generic subsystems, they tend to have the same change dynamic as the subsystem they represent. Thus, managers demonstrate both change orientation and resistance to change, depending upon the subsystem they represent.

Regardless of the size of the organization, all of these generic functions are present in some form. Larger organizations will have many defined departments and individuals serving these functions. In smaller organizations, even with one or two employees, these functions must be provided. Thus, with fewer people, employees must carry multiple generic function responsibilities.

Organizational Products and Services

Up to this point, this book has emphasized the commonality of managerial functions. A review of the five case studies finds both similarities and differences required by these management positions. It is evident these managers (Lead Mechanic, Lead Production Superintendent, Manufacturing Superintendent, Dean of Academic Administration, and Restaurateur) engage in common practices which are basic to all management positions regardless of the specialty. They all supervise people; plan and organize processes; anticipate and solve problems; resolve conflicts; communicate with superiors, peers, and subordinates; set priorities; lead and attend meetings; and motivate employees, to mention a few commonalities. These common responsibilities, once understood, can guide you to more quickly cope with the scope of challenges you must address in your management career.

However, your organization's products and services greatly influence the specifics of your managerial challenges. Supervising engine mechanics, preparing a jet fighter for flight, managing a manufacturing process, registering students, keeping a restaurant profitable demand specific knowledge, skills, and experience related to that job. These specialized capacities are required by the products/services and the processes needed to accomplish the various tasks/responsibilities. Because of this, the knowledge needed by managers in a specific industry is also different and thus influences how the common functions of the manager are applied.

Overseeing the preparation of airplanes for flight requires a different set of knowledge and skills than does managing a restaurant or registering college students, as illustrated by the job descriptions of managers presented in the case studies. Though managers perform common functions, the specifics of how they carry out these functions are modified by the nature of the products and services they oversee. Learning these specifics and modifying the common managerial functions to fit these needs occur through formal education, personal experience, and on-the-job training.

Organizations are developed to provide products and/or services to their customers. These products/services are provided through the productive subsystems of each organization. There are literally millions of products/services offered by organizations and making sense of these offerings is challenging. One approach to simplifying these products/services is the classification of organizational content as object molding, object processing, people processing, or people molding/changing.[3]

Object molding organizations manufacture things. They start with physical materials and mold them into products. Their processes and technologies focus on taking materials and transforming them into products through such molding techniques as forming, cutting, bending and pressing, drilling, shaping, and assembling. Examples of object molding are manufacturing firms, such as automobile production, building construction, and clothing manufacturing.

Object processing organizations take already produced products and offer them for sale to customers. They do not manufacture goods but "process" these goods for distribution and/or sale to customers. They reach out to their customers through a multitude of distribution modes, presenting their products for inspection. Some examples include furniture outlets, clothing stores, grocery stores, auto sales, and on-line catalog sales. Thus, any organization which wholesales or retails goods for sale falls into the object processing category.

People processing organizations focus on delivering services to people based upon some general objective criteria either required by law or a purchase, which entitles the person to the service. For example, the Social Security Administration processes an applicant's request for benefits according to preset criteria, assessing what benefits the applicant qualifies for, determining the dollar benefits due the applicant, and then awarding the prescribed benefit in an objective manner. Other examples include amusement parks, movie theaters, Department of Motor Vehicles, and public transportation systems.

People molding/changing organizations are engaged in activities aimed at significantly changing the physical, personal, social, and/or spiritual characteristics of the individual. Examples include education, health maintenance, and therapeutic/rehabilitative organizations.

All organizations do not fit neatly into these four descriptive categories but the classification helps in focusing on what organizations do. Some organizations may show blends of these types. For example, Disney World processes people but can also claim people changing qualities such as educational and restorative (relaxation, tension reduction) qualities. Whether the organization focuses on molding/processing objects or processing/changing people has an important impact on the manner in which the organization views its customers and employees.

Object molding/processing is impersonal and can lead to treating customers and employees in the same impersonal manner. Objects are non-responsive and easily manipulated into the desired forms and orders. This tends to cultivate managerial assumptions about handling customers and employees in similar fashion. On the other hand, people processing/changing organizations deal with people who are responsive, reactive, and involved in receiving the service. Human beings have attitudes, opinions, and expectations of the services and are not hesitant in expressing their opinions about how the services should be delivered. These characteristics tend to make this type of organization much more attentive to and reactive to people. This same attitude can translate into similar concerns about employees, making management more sensitive to the needs, feelings, and opinions of employees.

Managers in object molding/processing organizations must resist treating customers and employees in impersonal non-responsive manners and recognize they are not objects but people. Managers of people processing/changing organizations must resist becoming overly involved in the personal problems of their customers such that they lose professionalism and run their organizations in inefficient ways.

In addition to understanding the general themes above, you should, at the very least, have a general knowledge of the basic products/services provided by your organization. The depth of knowledge of the products/services is to some degree related to the specific position you occupy. Managers directly involved in the production of the products/services will need to know the details of the production processes, and monitor procedures and quality standards. On the other hand, managers heading supportive responsibilities such as accounting, human resources, maintenance, buildings and grounds, need not have an in-depth knowledge of the organization's products/services. However, functions with intermediate involvement will need enough product/service knowledge to support the production process or enough technical knowledge to sell the product/service to customers. Thus, the depth of product/service knowledge needed by a specific manager will vary depending upon the area of responsibility.

Your Future in Management

"Publically recognizing your subordinates' contributions does not detract from your reputation but rather enhances your relationships with your peers and subordinates."

Lee E. Jacokes

This book presented a selection of topics introducing some concepts and challenges of management. These topics were selected because they represent some of the typical knowledge and issues new managers face early in their management experience. However, there are many more challenges to be faced, many more skills to be mastered, and much knowledge to be learned. In fact, as with any profession, it is true to say that becoming a good manager is a career long process and that one's learning never is completed.

Just how far one desires to climb in management is limited by one's motivation, education, and experience. The higher up the management ladder one goes, the more likely formal education and extensive experience will be required. However, in many ways the sky is the limit. Effective managers are at a premium and those who prepare themselves and develop a reputation as an effective manager are always in demand. Advancement comes when preparation and opportunity meet. Thus, preparing one's self for future opportunities is mandatory.

Management Challenges

So, following are some parting ideas about management challenges and how you might consider addressing them.

Change from Specialist to Manager. As mentioned earlier, most of us enter management because we showed talent as a specialist, attracting the attention of our fellow workers and superiors, and then were asked to take on some management responsibility. Perhaps our first management position allowed us to both manage and keep up with our specialist duties. However, an insidious transformation begins at that point. Like a caterpillar transforming into a butterfly, whether the caterpillar likes it or not, the specialist begins the metamorphosis to a manager. The longer one serves as a manager and the higher up in management one goes have a profound effect on this transformation.

Since management involves learning new skills and knowledge, mastering them requires focus which takes one away from keeping up with the original specialty. This often results in a gradual loss of specialist competencies. Limits are placed on one's ability to keep up with the evolving knowledge, emerging technologies, and skills needed to remain a competent specialist. At some point, the specialist turned manager begins to realize he/she is being left behind by the changing specialty. Thus, a decision about which world he/she wishes to remain in must be made: the specialty or management.

Manager of a Specialty. Throughout this book, the commonality of management across specialties was emphasized. However, management of specific specialties requires some knowledge of the particular characteristics of the specialty. Whether one manages engineers, teachers, manufacturing workers, medical personnel, etc., the knowledge of the specialty is important to being a successful specialty manager. Although each specialty shares in the common knowledge and processes of all managers, educating one's self in the specific managerial knowledge, techniques, and technologies of the specialty is important.

There are many resources available to specialty managers which can educate them to the special characteristics, technologies, and processes unique to the field. Publications are available for nearly every specialty, e.g., educational administration, engineering management, hospital management, marketing management. In fact one only needs to search the internet for a specialty by listing its name followed by the word "management" or "administration" to access information specifically addressing the managerial needs of that specialty. Many of the ideas presented in this book will be repeated in these materials; however, the unique managerial needs of the specialty will also be covered.

Mentors. New managers should form relationships with experienced managers who are willing and able to serve as mentors. Mentors are wise, experienced, and trusted professionals who are willing and able to act as a confidential helper and guide to another manager. They assist new managers in their professional development by discussing their career plans, helping them evaluate options and achievements, and working through issues encountered by the new manager. Mentors are people willing to help other managers learn from their experience. Having a mentor provides the fledgling manager with someone who can serve as teacher and sounding board.

Mentors can be found within the organization, frequently already known by the new manager. Some organizations have programs in which they have identified willing mentors and encourage managers to form mentor/mentee relationships. Also, there are professional management coaches who can be contracted in this capacity.

Formal Education and Training. Nearly every community has formal educational opportunities to continue one's management training. Degree programs at the bachelor, master, and even PhD degree levels are available depending upon the new manager's previous education level and interest. Currently, most of these programs offer day and evening classes, and distance learning (internet) formats tailored to fit the working professional's schedule.

There is also managerial training offered by local employment associations, Chambers of Commerce, professional associations such as the American Management Association, etc. Such offerings are often in the form of seminars, workshops, and lectures, often awarding Continuing Education (CE) units of achievement.

Depending upon the organization, manager training may be offered in several formats, as mentioned above, including formal management training which exposes new managers to a variety of departments and functions within the organization. Many organizations offer tuition reimbursement benefits for those pursuing formal management education. Contact with your organization's Human Resources Department to ask about such financial support is recommended.

Informal Training Sources. There is a nearly unlimited fund of information available to the motivated manager willing to seek out more education. Sources to be considered include: public libraries, college and university libraries and bookstores, commercial bookstores, and the internet.

Libraries. Nearly any public library has a wide selection of management publications covering many aspects of management. In addition, Community Colleges, four year colleges and universities, all have extensive library resources including books, videos, audio recordings, and other training resources. Usually, this information is available to the community even if not a registered student.

Bookstores. Any commercial bookstore will have an extensive management section of publications covering management thinking. Other publication sources are college and university bookstores. Purchasing textbooks used in business and management courses is an excellent way of accessing a broad range of management information.

The Internet. The internet provides an almost limitless source of management information. This includes management summaries, specific management topics, and access to internet courses offered by colleges and universities, private consultants, and many free sources. A recent Google search found 206 million hits under the term management education while the term managerial planning produced 6.5 million hits. Searching for specific topics, the internet can provide quick access to these topics from one's desk.

Social Importance of Management

Managers spend most of their efforts focusing on their immediate responsibilities of directing their departments/units. However, there is a broader importance of their efforts. They contribute to the larger society through their efforts to bring products and services to meet societal needs. Society is maintained and developed through the collective efforts of its organizations.

Whether managers serve in organizations which produce tangible products; serve in the maintenance functions of education, health, and restorative processes; serve in political/governmental services; or serve the many other needs of society, their efforts matter.

To be an effective manager is a socially valuable calling. Managers are given an honored position in society. However, they must remember it is only temporary. How the manager uses the power granted to him/her is critical to the success of his/her efforts. Superiors grant the manager the formal power needed to carry out the job responsibilities while subordinates grant the manager the personal power of consent and admiration to lead them. How well the manager handles these two power sources/gifts will determine the manager's effectiveness and success or failure. Effective, ethical, motivated, and socially responsible managers are necessary for the continued well being of society.

Becoming a good manager requires learning, experience, and dedication. To a great extent it requires development of character.

References

1. Schein, E. H. (2010). *Organizational culture and leadership.* San Francisco, CA: Jossey-Bass.

2. French, J. R. P., & Raven, B. (1959). The bases of social power. In D. Cartwright (Ed.), Studies in social power (pp. 150-167). Ann Arbor: University of Michigan Press.

3. Katz, D., & Kahn. R. L. (1978). *The social psychology of organizations.* New York, NY: Jon Wiley & Sons.

4. Mintzberg, H. (1973). *The nature of managerial work.* New York, NY: Harper & Row.

5. Katz, R. I. (1955). Skill of an effective administrator. *Harvard Business Review*, January-February, 33-42.

6. Weaver, W., & Shannon, C. E. (1963). *The mathematical theory of communication.* Champaign: University of Illinois Press.

7. Fayol, H. (1925). *Industrial and general administration.* Paris, France: Dunod.

8. Taylor, F. W. (1911). *The principles of scientific management.* New York, NY: Harper Bros.

9. Roethlisberger, F. J., & Dickson, W. J. (1939). *Management and the worker.* Cambridge, MA: Harvard University Press.

10. Simon, H. (1991). Bounded rationality and organizational learning. *Organization Science 2*(1), 125-134.

11. Fisher, R., & Ury, W. (1992). *Getting to yes: Negotiating agreement without giving in* (2nd ed.). Boston, MA: Houghton Mifflin.

12. Stogdill, R. M. (1974). *Handbook of leadership: A survey of the literature.* New York, NY: Free Press.

13. Bennis, W., & Nanus, B. (1986). *Leaders.* New York, NY: Harper and Row.

14. Hersey, P., Blanchard, K., & Johnson, D. (2008). *Management of organizational behavior: Leading human resources* (9th ed.). Upper Saddle River, NJ: Pearson Education.

15. Greenleaf, R. K. (1978). *Servant: Leader and follower.* New York, NY: Paulist Press.

16. Maslow, A. (1954). *Motivation and personality.* New York, NY: Harper.

17. McClelland, D. (1987). *Human motivation.* New York, NY: Cambridge University Press.

18. Skinner, B. F. (1953). *Science and human behavior.* New York, NY: Macmillan.

19. Benne, K., & Sheats, P. (1948). Functional roles of group members. *Journal of Social Issues, 4,* 41-49.

20. Deming, W. E. (1986). *Out of the crisis.* Cambridge, MA: MIT Press.

Acknowledgements

Although writing a book is a solitary process, it is also immensely improved by the critical review of others. I thank the following family members, friends, and colleagues for their generous readings of my efforts and their suggestions for improvements.

Kim M. Bintz
Jeannine S. Jacokes
Robert Kunnen, PhD
Ric Miller
Paul Pearson, PhD
Pat Weisbeck

I also wish to thank the five managers upon whom the case studies were based. Though they wished to remain anonymous, their management experience helped to bring real life examples of the challenges of management.

A special thanks is due Cathy Weisbeck, PhD, who edited my musings. She took my "perfect draft" and turned it into readable English, suggesting better organization and idea flow, thus, greatly improving the presentation.

Finally, thanks to Francene, for a life time of support, acceptance, and love.